CONTENTS

CW00363672

ACKNOWLEDGEMENTS

Prison Reform Trust is grateful to Barclays Plc for supporting this unique study of prison education from the prisoners' perspective.

The Time to Learn research project has been guided by an expert Advisory Group chaired by Professor Gus John.

Two independent research associates, Julia Braggins and Jenny Talbot, undertook the study on behalf of Prison Reform Trust supported by Kimmett Edgar, Research Manager, PRT and PRT volunteer, Cecilia Yardley.

We are most grateful for the support of the prisons involved in this study and thank prisoners, education and prison staff for their time, friendship and help given to us during our visits. We should also like to thank the Offenders learning and Skills Unit at the Department for Education and Science for its assistance throughout this study.

FOREWORD

At its best, prison education can open up opportunities, enlighten people, broaden their horizons and build their self-confidence. It can increase their awareness of options, giving them a real choice of a life away from crime. Education can open up the legitimate means of achieving success.

But this raises the issue of the educational experience of prisoners prior to custody. A lack of education constitutes a bar to full participation in society as a valued and productive citizen. Half of all prisoners do not have the skills required by 96 per cent of jobs. As this report makes clear, education can also exclude people when what is offered does not fit the needs, interests, the culture or the lifestyle of the person to whom it is provided.

Prison education is, for many, a second chance to learn the skills and social competences they will need in order to be reintegrated. But there is a catch: that education is offered in an institution which by its very nature isolates still further many who are already excluded from society. Imprisonment widens the gap between those people and mainstream society and brands them in a manner that compounds their social exclusion.

Time to Learn explores the prisoners' experience of education – the benefits and drawbacks of learning in a prison environment, the relevance of the curriculum to their diverse needs, the range of resources available and the limitations imposed upon learning by prison routines.

The prisoners in this study suggest, in different ways, that the education department is an oasis of humanity in an otherwise cold and impersonal environment. Certainly education should play a vital role in preparing prisoners for reintegration upon release, but it is doubtful how many offenders regard this as a realistic aspiration.

This study represents people in prison as an indispensable source of first-hand information about learning experiences in custody: the ways that prison education can transform lives and the obstacles posed to learning development by the prison environment.

I welcome this report because it brings the views of prisoners to bear on the debate regarding the nature of prison education. If prison education is to meet the needs of offenders in custody, then it is essential that we learn what those needs are. If prison education is to be part of the 'Learning Revolution', in the knowledge-based economy, and empower people with the knowledge and skills so that they can become responsible members of society, then an obvious first step is to consult prisoners, respecting their unique perspective on the kinds of services required and the quality of current provision. *Time to Learn* provides a prism through which policy makers and practitioners could develop a vision of the future role and organisation of prison education.

Professor Gus John
Chair of the Advisory Group
October 2003

INTRODUCTION

"Our vision is that offenders according to need should have access to education and training both in prisons and in the community, which enables them to gain the skills and qualifications they need to hold down a job and have a positive role in society, and that the content and quality of learning programmes in prisons, and the qualifications to which these lead, are the same as comparable provision in the community." [1]

But what do prisoners think about education in prisons? What have their experiences been? What might they recommend for the future of prison education? Despite a great deal of interest in prison education, the voices of prisoners are rarely heard. To our knowledge, there have been few studies that set out with the sole intention of eliciting prisoners' views about their experience of education in prison.

Against a background that places the consumer at the very heart of public service reform, the Prison Reform Trust (PRT), supported by Barclays, decided to gather prisoners' views on prison education and to use that information to influence change. More than simply a 'consumer satisfaction survey', *Time to Learn* explores the perceptions of prisoner-learners drawing on their experiences and their ideas to develop a wide range of recommendations for prison education. From the immediate and the practical through to longer-term changes in policy and culture, the recommendations drawn from this study are based on the views of prisoners.

I.   Background

We felt it was important to look at the wider context in which prison education takes place: the delivery of prisoner education; its aims; the curriculum; funding; the impact of overcrowding; prisoners' previous experience of education; and other research on the topic.

• The Delivery of Prisoner Education

The publication of this report coincides with significant and rapid developments in prison education and training policy and funding. The structure and management of education in prisons has changed dramatically over the last 10 years. In 1993, prison education, which had formerly been delivered through local education authorities, was contracted out on a five yearly basis to colleges of further education and other external providers. Currently 28 external providers, including 25 colleges of further education, two local education authorities and one private company, are delivering education in prisons. Existing contracts will be re-tendered in April 2004.

The wide variety of providers can affect the continuity of a prisoner's learning career, as their time in prison may involve a number of transfers from one establishment to another.

The provision of education was directed by the Prisoners' Learning and Skills Unit, created in April 2001. In May 2003, the Unit was given additional responsibility for probation education and training policy and development and renamed the Offenders' Learning and Skills Unit (OLSU).

---

1 DfES/PLSU (2003) Improving Offenders' Learning and Skills Delivery Plan 2003/4 - 2004/5.

A strategic partnership between the Department for Education and Skills (DfES) and the Prison Service generated a delivery plan for 2003/04-2005/06, *Improving Offenders' Learning and Skills*. The plan calls for a range of changes in the way education in prison is to be delivered, including:

- The redesign and re-tendering of education contracts for all prison establishments, including the incorporation of vocational training in contracts from April 2004
- A major review of the prison curriculum
- Increased funding for prison education of 47 per cent over the next three years, from £85 million this year to £125 million in 2005/06
- Developing criteria and arrangements for a Standards Fund to improve the quality of learning and skills provision.

Under the delivery plan the OLSU is committed to providing education in prison to as equal standard as could be gained outside. Consistent with this aim, prison education will be subject to the same inspection regimes as for mainstream education including visits from the Adult Learning Inspectorate and Ofsted as well as from Her Majesty's Chief Inspector of Prisons.

As with most public service provision, Key Performance Targets (KPTs) are a feature of prison education. National targets are set for Basic and Key skills at entry level and for levels 1 and 2 and disaggregated between individual prisons. (Level 1 represents the educational skill level expected of an 11 year old child.) Performance against them is monitored on a monthly basis. For the year ending March 2003, targets for Basic and Key Skills for the 118 prisons for which figures were available were exceeded by 44 per cent, a major achievement. However, 35 prisons failed in one or more target areas. [2]

• Aims

> "Education is an important factor in reducing re-offending. The work we are doing in our prisons to rehabilitate, educate and prepare offenders for their return to society is critical in providing them with an alternative to crime." [3]

Writing for *The Independent*, Lord Dearing, who chaired the National Committee of Inquiry into Higher Education, put it like this:

> "Whatever the basis for getting prisoners' commitment to education, the potential return through reduced reoffending rates by people who can hold down a decent job is compelling." [4]

The aim of the DfES, which, it must be assumed, applies as much to prisoners as to the rest of the population is:

> "To help build a competitive economy and inclusive society by:
> Creating opportunities for everyone to develop their learning
> Releasing potential in people to make the most of themselves
> Achieving excellence in standards of education and level of skills." [5]

Creating opportunities, releasing potential and achieving excellence are certainly as relevant to prison education as to any other educational provision. And yet at any given time only one third of prisoners have access to education.

---

2 Personal communication from OLSU, 2003.

3 DfES/PLSU (2003).

4 Ron Dearing (2002) 'Education should be the key to prisoners' freedom,' The Independent, 25 July 2002.

5 DfES (2002) 'Education and Skills: Delivering Results - A Strategy to 2006.

The executive summary to the OLSU delivery plan acknowledges some of the difficulties of the prison regime:

- A historical lack of priority given to education and training
- The sudden movement of prisoners during courses
- Lower pay for prisoners to undertake education than to work
- Separate planning and delivery of education and training in most establishments.[6]

Some of these issues are already being tackled – vocational training is to be incorporated in education contracts from April 2004 and there is no doubt that a greater priority is now being given to education in prisons. As to sudden movement and lower pay, it must be hoped that these will be given the same priority in the very near future.

The OLSU delivery plan (DfES/Prison Service, 2003) aspires to a joined up approach to offender education from within the constraints of the prison to the wider community. It sets out a commitment:

> *"...to explore ways in which we can make learning for offenders more continuous, cohesive and more aligned with provision for learners in mainstream education."*

Yet, according to *Shared Responsibilities*, a report jointly published by NATFHE and the Association of Colleges:

> *"Only one third of education managers said that they regularly receive prisoners' records following transfers."*[7]

The study set out to gain prisoners' views on the extent to which such continuity was achieved in their experience (between one prison and another, but also between prison and the outside community). The ideal of a seamless link between learning inside and outside prison should be a key part of effective resettlement. We recognised the importance of a seamless provision of education and sought the views of prisoners on the extent to which they believed that their in-prison education would lead to improved educational opportunities outside.

According to the Social Exclusion Unit report, *Reducing re-offending by ex-prisoners*, "...as few as six per cent of prisoners have an education or training place to go to on release." The SEU report concludes that: "Without very clear and well-supported routes into learning, any progress made in prison will end on release."[8]

The introduction of the joint prison/probation offender assessment system, OASys, may help. OASys is an IT-based risk/needs assessment tool, shared between and accessible to both the National Probation Service and the Prison Service. It seeks to better inform and enhance sentence planning, including in part a focus on education and training. Following pilots, OASys will start in early 2004 and has the potential to join up the information flow and service provision for the individual prisoner before, after and during their sentence. The responsibility for implementing OASys within the Prison Service will rest with prison officers.

6 PLSU (2002) 'Prisoners Learning and Skills Delivery Plan: Executive Summary'.

7 Julia Braggins (2002) Shared Responsibilities: Education for prisoners at a time of change, NATFHE and the Association of Colleges.

8 Social Exclusion Unit (2002) Reducing re-offending by ex-prisoners, London: SEU.

• **Curriculum**

According to the OLSU's website:

> "The main thrust of education in prisons is to provide opportunities for offenders to attain a
> range of nationally recognised qualifications up to level 2, and in some cases beyond, which
> will enhance their employability on release. All prisons must provide a core curriculum, which
> includes:
>   • Initial assessment
>   • National Record of Achievement
>   • Basic Skills
>   • Key Skills
>   • English for speakers of other languages
>   • Information and Communications Technology
>   • Social and Life Skills
>   • Generic preparation for work." [9]

According to *Shared Responsibilities*, less than half of prison governors, education managers
and providers of prison education were satisfied with the curriculum in terms of its relevance
to the needs of prisoners.

The report states that, "The narrowing of the curriculum was the shared concern of
governors, education managers and providers of prison education". A particular issue for
many was the omission of the creative arts. As one respondent put it:

> "The curriculum broadly ignores the positive contribution creative education – e.g. art,
> music, dance and drama – can have when dealing with very damaged individuals with low
> self esteem ... and a low opinion of formal education." [10]

The OLSU delivery plan is committed to:

> "... undertaking a major review of the prison curriculum, ensuring that it is developed in line
> with government priorities both within the FE/Adult learning sectors and the criminal
> justice system."

• **Funding**

Total funding for prisoner education in 2002/03 totalled £66.7m, out of which teaching costs,
educational materials and library costs were met. The 2002 Spending Review increased
funding for prison education and figures for the next three years, in millions, stand at £85M for
2003-4; £110M for 2004-5; and £125M for 2005-6. In addition, funding for vocational training
of £12M per year for the three years, ring-fenced from 2003/04, will transfer to the OLSU. A
further £20M from the Capital Modernisation Fund is being allocated to prisons for
improvements to learning facilities. [11]

Despite these investments, prisoner-learners have always been the poor relation when
compared to other adult learners. Even with the recent increase in spending and the promise
of more to come, the 2002-3 average of £1,185 per prisoner (based on the Certified Normal
Accommodation – CNA – spend per head as at 31 March 2002, in 122 establishments)
remains less than half the average cost of secondary school education at £2,590 per student
per year, which many prisoners will have missed.

With the creation in 2001 of the PLSU came ring-fenced budgets for education but not for
vocational training. Lord Dearing wrote in *The Independent*:

> "The cut of 50% in recent years in the provision for training in the construction trades
> reported by the Government's Social Exclusion Unit seems nothing short of perverse". [13]

9 Offenders Learning and Skills Unit website (2003) 'Initiatives: Curriculum, Key Facts,' (see also: Prison Service Order 4205, June 2000).
10 Braggins (2002).   11 DfES/PLSU (2003).
12 DfES (2001) Statistical Bulletin, 'Education and Training Expenditure since 1991-1992.   13 Ron Dearing (2002).

There are also significant disparities in education funding per head among prisons. Funding has been allocated primarily on the basis of spending patterns largely determined by the number of teaching hours ordered in the past by establishments. This has meant that prisons delivering the same core curriculum with similar types of prisoners have received very different funding allocations.

The amount of spend per head across the prison estate for 2002/03 ranges from as little as £195 (HMP Latchmere House, Category C/D Resettlement) to £5,707 (HMP & YOI Hatfield, Open YOI) with an average spend of £1,185. (Spend per head is based on CNA as at 31 March 2002. [14])

In this study, eight out of the twelve prisons spent below the average spend per head. The local prisons tended to feature low per prisoner spend, while the YOI was above the national average as was one of the two women's prisons visited. For HMP Parc, spend per head is not available because it is a matter of 'commercial confidentiality'. The amount per head spent by eleven of the twelve prisons in this study for the year to March 2003 is shown below:

Table One: Spending levels on education in the prisons visited

Establishment	Category	Spend per head* (£)
Aylesbury	YOI for Long Term offenders	1454
Askham Grange	Female open training and YOI	1350
Downview	Female closed	964
Guys Marsh	Closed category C YOI and prison	891
Leicester	Category B local prison	1815
Long Lartin	Training/Dispersal prison	759
Manchester	Local prison	805
Parc	Category B local prison	N/A
Pentonville	Local prison	530
Wakefield	Dispersal/Lifer main centre	794
Wandsworth	Category B local prison	455
Wellingborough	Category C training prison	876

*Spend per head based on CNA as at 31 March 2002

According to the SEU report, cited above:

> "The inequality of funding between prisons with similar roles is a key barrier to raising standards of education."

The SEU report goes on to say that whilst the OLSU will address this issue, "the challenge is considerable."

The OLSU delivery plan requires prisons in future to have in place, "three year development plans to raise achievement levels and improve education and training outcomes for prisoners" on which funding will be dependent.

• Learners in prison

> "In any one year, 130,000 people are or have been in prison, with a further 200,000 supervised by the Probation Service in the community. Around 50% of these individuals have poor reading skills, 66% have poor numeracy skills, and a staggering 81% of prisoners have writing skills below Level 1. This is a serious obstacle to the rehabilitation of ex-offenders and to their search for employment once they leave prison." [15]

14 Personal communication from OLSU, 2003.
15 OLSU website, 'Initiatives: Basic Skills, Key Facts.'

Over the last three years the prison population has increased by 10 per cent. The prison population as at 11 July 2003 was 74,012 (an increase of 2,532 on the previous year), compared with a CNA (the in use uncrowded capacity of the prison estate) of 66,101 and an Operational Capacity (maximum safe overcrowded capacity of the prison estate) of 76,405.[16]

According to recent Home Office statistics, further growth of between 28 and 54 per cent can be expected. This will increase the prison population to a minimum of 91,400 and a maximum of 109,600 by 2009. The figures predict a continued rise in the number of sentenced women prisoners and sentenced young offenders, which are expected to grow by some 76 per cent and 41 per cent respectively to 2009.[17]

At the same time as the population has increased, it is a major accomplishment that the amount of time spent by prisoner-learners attending education classes has also increased in recent years. In 2000, prisoner-learners in local prisons spent an average of 4.86 hours per week attending education classes and 8.23 hours per week in open prisons.[18] According to OLSU figures, just under one third of the prison population is attending education classes. The Home Office Resettlement Survey 2001 found that nearly 50 per cent of prisoners attended some form of education and training during their time in prison.

• *Prisoners' educational backgrounds*

The education offered to prisoners must necessarily take into account their previous experience, and this means that problems in education in the wider social context are important. The DfES acknowledges that the current system "has significant weaknesses"[19].

According to Mike Tomlinson, Chair of the Learning Trust, the "significant weaknesses" of the current system impact particularly on "key groups such as white boys from lower socio-economic backgrounds, black boys, children in public care and refugee children." [20]

Whilst every other black and minority ethnic group made progress in attainment at secondary level in the period 2000-02, Mike Tomlinson notes:

> *"The proportion of Afro-Caribbean teenagers achieving at least five good GCSE grades actually fell between 2000 and 2002 from 39% to 36%."*

The DfES also acknowledged that "too many young people lose interest in learning before the age of 16." In the summary to *14-19: opportunities and excellence*, the DfES states:

> *"This disengagement from learning is often just the beginning of a cycle of low expectations and disaffection, with consequences felt not only by individuals but by local communities and wider society."* [21]

Many prisoners, although by no means all, come into custody with a history of educational under-achievement and poor skills. The SEU report, *Reducing re-offending by ex-prisoners*, presented a disturbing picture of the educational level of the prison population. Prisoners are over twenty times more likely than the general population to have been excluded from school; and ten times as likely to have been a regular truant. Further, the SEU found that half of all prisoners were at or below Level 1 (the level expected of an 11 year old) in reading; two-thirds in numeracy; and four-fifths in writing. [22]

The SEU report also notes that specific groups are likely to be disadvantaged by prison education, including black and minority ethnic prisoners, people on remand, women, and young prisoners:

> *"Black prisoners tend to be more highly qualified than white prisoners, and so benefit relatively less from the emphasis on improving prisoners' basic skills."*

16 RDS (2002) 'Prison Population Brief, England and Wales, December 2002.
17 RDS (2002) Projections of long term trends in the prison population to 2009. 18 Prison Statistics England and Wales 2000, 2001.
19 DfES (2003). 20 Mike Tomlinson (2003) 'Learning for all: can it be made a reality?' RSA Journal, June 2003.
21 DfES (2003) 14-19: opportunities and excellence, DfES.
22 Social Exclusion Unit (2002) Reducing re-offending by ex-prisoners, London: The Social Exclusion Unit.

"Although one in two remands go on to receive a custodial sentence they often have little opportunity to attend education and training."

"Women prisoners are particularly likely to have poor education history and few qualifications.

A quarter (of young adult prisoners) will have terminated their education by the time they are aged 14."

Thus, the DfES objective to, "enable all young people to develop and to equip themselves with the skills, knowledge and personal qualities needed for life and work" is particularly relevant to prison education, making up for what many prisoners will have missed in secondary school education. But the DfES' commitment to increased participation in higher education and fair access is not reflected in practice and in performance targets for prison education.

At the other end of the scale, there are highly qualified prisoners who both enjoyed and did well at school, many of whom would like to continue their education. There are prisoners who seize the opportunity for what they see as a second chance at education and who excel. The massive range of ability, motivation, prior learning experience and attainment presented by prisoners, together with the prison regime within which prison education takes place, make for a unique and often less than satisfactory experience, for prisoner-learners and education staff alike.

A 'one size fits all' approach to education cannot work. The recent DfES publication, *14-19: opportunity and excellence*, promises to transform education and training through the introduction of more flexibility into the system and by placing the needs of the learner at the centre of provision. Placing the needs of the individual prisoner at the centre of prison education and creating flexibility of provision would therefore be consistent with mainstream education. In order for prisoners to develop the skills, knowledge and personal qualities necessary to manage effectively both inside prison and on release, a wide range of different opportunities that reflect the diverse needs of the prison population is fundamental. Simply offering more of the same in terms of a relatively inflexible, academically inclined, school-based curriculum will not work. And that has implications for education staff, too. The need to recruit and retain high quality education staff, supported by a structured programme of continuing professional development and a rigorous inspection framework would seem to be integral to ensuring progress.

• Previous research on the topic

Time to Learn builds on a range of studies into prison education.

For example, *Shared Responsibilities*, published in January 2002 jointly by NATFHE and the Association of Colleges, presents an overview of the perceptions of prison governors, education managers and contractors on the state of prison education in England and Wales.

A high priority for Government is to establish links between prison education and a reduced risk of reoffending upon release. The SEU report cited above states bluntly that, "Prisoners attending education and training are less likely to re-offend." The report lists some of the specific benefits:

"Raising educational and skills levels has a positive impact on employability, a key factor in reducing re-offending. It can also improve self-esteem and motivation, as well as reducing the likelihood that their [prisoners'] own children will struggle at school."

The high proportion of prisoners in need of basic education also shapes the type of provision that is made available. A recent study by Claudia Gosse, Is *education valued in the prison?* notes:

> *"The emphasis placed on basic skills ... reflects the growing awareness of the difficulties caused by lack of these skills, and government targets are based on this."* [23]

Gosse refers to research undertaken by the London University Institute of Education which:

> *"...establishes for the first time a firm link between crime and poor basic skills. Raising standards of literacy and numeracy won't lead to a crime free society, but it will make it less likely that frustration and failure result in criminality."*

A different view is argued by David Wilson, in an article, Valuing prisoner education:

> *"Whilst no one would deny that there is a great deal of evidence to suggest that basic literacy and numeracy skills are lacking in some of the prison population – especially those on remand – a policy based solely on this approach implicitly suggests that those with literacy and numeracy skills do not commit crime, and leads to a void in regime provision for development beyond this level. In short art, drama and vocational classes start to disappear and it becomes even harder to work towards higher educational achievement."* [24]

The role of the arts in prison remains contested. The arts are seen by some as a soft option. For prisoners who have rejected, or have been rejected by, formal education the arts can provide a route back into learning. A report published by the Prison Reform Trust sheds some light on the importance of arts education in prisons:

> *"Arts activities then are more concerned with internal goals – development of the 'self', communication, respect – than with external goals – gaining qualifications, or skills directly applicable to employment or survival. Progress cannot be demonstrated as easily as examination results. Achievements are more subtle, more psychological and more difficult to put into words."* [25]

Thinking about how prisoners view the possible benefits of arts in prison already begins to move us away from an image of prisoners as passive recipients to seeing them as active in their learning experience.

Prison(er) Education is a powerful collection of 'Tales of Change and Transformation' that demonstrates the huge diversity in prisoners as learners. Emma Hughes, a contributor, draws on prisoners' letters, written to the Prisoners' Education Trust, to highlight positive effects of education:

> *"Having a meaningful course to study is a great help in coping with prison life."*

> *"Forms and tests have always frightened me, so I find this new experience really beneficial to me."*

> *"I just really wish more people were able to take education seriously in prison. It really is the only place you feel both human and confident. Achievement I believe is the best possible form of rehabilitation."* [26]

In another chapter in the same volume, Anne Reuss and David Wilson advocate an emphasis on prisoner, as opposed to prison, education:

> *"...the implications are quite profound if applied both in theory and practice. Prisoner education is about people learning in a particular setting – a prison setting – and once that distinction is made, education programmes in prisons can be seen as something that may offer benefits and opportunities to individual prisoners – as people."*

23 Claudia Gosse (2002) Is education valued in prisons? unpublished MA thesis, University of Southampton.

24 David Wilson (2001) 'Valuing prisoner education,' The Prison Report, No. 54, 18-19.

25 Nick Flynn and David Price, 'Education in Prisons - A National Survey, Prison Reform Trust, 1995.

26 David Wilson and Anne Reuss, eds (2000) Prison(er) Education: Stories of Change and Transformation, Winchester: Waterside Press.

The present study was conducted in the same spirit, exploring the experience of people who are engaged in the process of learning, and happen to be in a prison environment.

2.   Aims of this study

The principal objective of *Time to Learn* was to elicit and explore prisoners' perceptions of education in prison in order to influence change. The study did not attempt to judge practice or to isolate specific issues for particular groups of prisoners, for example women prisoners, black and minority ethnic prisoners, younger and older prisoners, neither was it concerned with the purpose of education in prison.

A plethora of Government initiatives have urged providers of public services to establish the 'consumer' perception and to respond accordingly. And this is not simply about giving people what they want, regardless. It's about improving accessibility, enhancing the relevance and quality of service provision and above all it's about responding to consumer need, in this case, the needs of the prisoner-learner. If we don't know what the perception of the prisoner-learner is, how can we respond in a way that is both relevant to their needs and that encourages participation?

We did not set out to test hypotheses or to prove our own pre-conceived notions. Our goal has been to explore, appreciate and to present the perceptions of prisoner-learners of education in prison. Throughout the study, we have tried not to find-fault or to compare establishments. We have sought to adopt an "appreciative inquiry" stance recognising the very difficult environment in which education in prison frequently finds itself placed.

3.   Methods

• Sample

The study took place between January and May 2003. The scale was small, incorporating 12 prisons over six months. It involved listening to adult prisoners and young offenders, aged 18 – 21 years old. It was decided not to include juveniles in the study given their statutory entitlement to education and the consequent differences in provision such an entitlement brings. We conducted semi-structured group discussions with 8-10 prisoner-learners in each establishment and three to five prisoners not in education (henceforth 'NIE') in 10 prisons. In total, the report is drawn from the views expressed by 153 prisoners.

Participants in the research were recruited according to the purpose of the study; that is, the focus was on prisoner-learners. In selecting members of the discussion group, prisoners identified as being involved in education were those currently attending education classes provided by the education department. The NIE group were not attending education classes at the time we interviewed them, although some of them had attended prison education at some time in the past.

We were aware that different prisoner groups were likely to have experienced different issues and challenges in terms of education both inside prison and out. The prisoners who took part represented a wide range, including:
- Sentenced prisoners and those on remand
- Young offenders and adults
- Black and minority ethnic prisoners
- Women prisoners, and
- Security categories from open prisons to high security.

The selection of prisoners for our discussions was intended to avoid an imbalance of any specific kind of educational group. Of the 153 prisoners involved in the study:

- 16% were women
- 12% were young offenders
- 72% were adult men and
- 28% were from black and minority ethnic groups (this percentage was derived from a visible headcount in each of the discussion groups)

This compares with the prison population breakdown as at December 2002[27] of which:

- 6% were women
- 16% were young offenders
- 78% were adult men and
- 25% were from black and minority ethnic groups.

For each discussion our main contact at the individual prison, generally the education manager, was asked to gather a random cross-section of prisoner-learners and from this group to ask for volunteers. Although at most prisons this procedure was followed, it clearly wasn't in all. However at no prison did we believe that our sample had been hand-picked to offer the best response. For the NIE groups, a range of different methods were used, including the use of posters on the wings asking for volunteers, handing us over to prison officers deputised to find us a group from one of the workshops or on the wings, or arranging for a small group from a specific work area to join us in the education department, e.g. cleaners or gardeners.

• Definitions

In our discussions, prisoners were encouraged to consider education from a broad viewpoint – encouragement that was frequently pre-empted by prisoners themselves who volunteered examples and comment on a wide range of education that took place beyond the classroom. Indeed it was during our initial pilot discussion that one prisoner-learner suggested that to focus on education experienced purely within the classroom, as if in a vacuum away from the rest of the prison, would be to miss much of the learning that takes place throughout the prison. In as much as the prisoners themselves brought their perceptions of all of the following learning opportunities into our discussions, they are included in our definition of education for the purpose of this study:

- Classroom-based learning
- Distance learning
- Cell work, for example 'home work' or other self-motivated learning
- Vocational training, run by civilian prison staff
- Peer education/support, e.g. Toe by Toe
- Basic/key skills classes attached to workshops provided by the education department
- Gym-based learning, e.g. Learning through Sport run by prison PE instructors and at one of the prisons visited by a local university
- NVQs achieved through work, e.g. Industrial cleaning, kitchen work
- Offending behaviour programmes, run by the Psychology Department.

27 Prison Population Brief, England and Wales: December 2002, Veronica Hollis and Michelle Goodman, Research Development Statistics, London: Home Office.

The study is qualitative in that it is concerned with understanding nuances, motivations, attitudes and feelings. Occasionally we discovered that what we had been told by an individual prisoner or group of prisoners was not wholly accurate. Sometimes we already knew that what we were being told was inaccurate. But there is no reason to doubt that the individual prisoner (or the group) believed it to be true at that point in time.

Questionnaire

In *Shared Responsibilities*, governors, education managers and contractors raised a number of concerns on prisoners' behalf. These concerns helped to shape the key headings for our questionnaire on which this study is based. The subjects of interest include:

The importance of education:
- Why prisoners participate
- What they hope to get out of it
- Their experience of education in prison
- What's on offer?
- How it was decided which classes prisoners would attend
- Education and sentence planning
- The range and limitations of available opportunities
- Whether some groups of prisoners get priority or are left out

Facilities, teaching and learning preferences:
- The quality of the learning experience
- Prior learning experience
- What helps or hinders learning

Barriers and opportunities:
- Relevance of the curriculum
- Prisoner transfer between prisons
- Competing demands on prisoner time available for education
- Waiting lists

On release:
- The extent to which having participated in education might help on release
- Desire to continue education on release and perceived ease with which this might be possible
- Prisoner recommendations for the future of prison education.

We felt it important that the questionnaire was subject to feedback and our first prison visit, which was to HMP Wandsworth, provided that opportunity. Prisoner-learners at HMP Wandsworth both participated in a semi-structured discussion and provided feedback on the questionnaire, which subsequently informed its revision. The full questionnaire is at Appendix 2. A shorter version of this questionnaire was used for the NIE group.

For each discussion, one researcher worked through the questionnaire and managed the group dynamic, taking care to involve all participants, and the other researcher took notes. The note taker made every effort to record the voices of the prisoners in their own words, capturing verbatim the group's discussion. At the data gathering stage we were most careful simply to record and not to interpret.

The questionnaire was not designed with any one group in mind, although under section 5, which explored Barriers and Opportunities, we did ask specific questions in relation to particular groups, including women prisoners, black and minority ethnic prisoners, younger and older prisoners and prisoners who are also foreign nationals.

During the fieldwork, very little in the way of modification of the questionnaire took place, except in the important development of what we started to think of as the 'personal impact' agenda. In some of the discussions some prisoners began to volunteer information relative to their educational experiences of a more personal or sensitive nature than our questionnaire sought to elicit. For example about the more fundamental impact prison education had made on their lives, how it had changed their approach to family relationships or how a relationship with a particular tutor had changed the way they thought about things. We began to seek out such stories about the personal impact of the prison educational experience.

• *The prisons in the study*

A list of 15 prisons was identified on the basis of geographical spread and category, including male and female prisoners and young offenders, from which we hoped that 10 would agree to be part of the study. Our selection process was not based on any prior knowledge of the quality or range of educational provision in individual prisons. We deliberately decided not to try to select a mix of 'good' and 'improving' prison education departments. Appendix 3 shows the full list of prisons identified.

Judith Williams, Chief Education Officer, OLSU and member of the Advisory Group for the study, wrote to each of the identified prisons encouraging their participation, from which we received an immediate and positive response from 11 establishments. After conducting visits at roughly half of the prisons, it was decided that we should try again to arrange a visit to a dedicated YOI to ensure that the unique voice of the young offender would not be missed. And so HMYOI Aylesbury, one of our initial list of 15, was approached and agreed to join in the study.

Table Two: List of prisons visited in the study

Establishment	Category	CNA*	Location
HMP & YOI Askham Grange	Female open training	139	Yorkshire
HMYOI Aylesbury	Long-term YOI	348	Buckinghamshire
HMP Downview	Female closed	327	Surrey
HMP & YOI Guys Marsh	Closed category C YOI and prison	487	Dorset
HMP Leicester	Category B local prison	219	Leicestershire
HMP Long Lartin	Training/Dispersal prison	599	Worcestershire
HMP Manchester	Local prison	950	Manchester
HMP & YOI Parc	Category B local prison	800	Wales
HMP Pentonville	Local prison	897	London
HMP Wakefield	Dispersal/Lifer main centre	747	West Yorkshire
HMP Wandsworth	Category B local prison	1163	London
HMP Wellingborough	Category C training prison	526	Northamptonshire

*Certified Normal Accomodation (CNA) is the in use uncrowded capacity of the prison estate.

In all but two establishments, the responsibility for organising the visit was passed to the education department. The education manager generally welcomed us and introduced us to other members of the education team. At one prison we were invited to meet a governor who expressed a keen interest in the study and thanked us for giving her prison the opportunity to participate.

Positive relationships within the education staff team and between education and prison staff seemed to spill over into relationships with prisoner-learners. Where relationships appeared positive, we were better able to stimulate discussion. Where relationships were not so positive, it took a while longer to encourage free flowing discussion. At one prison, prisoner-learners spontaneously applauded the 'note taker' for her efforts.

At only one prison and in relation to only one prison officer did we feel that our efforts were being made light of when the prison officer concerned contrived – unsuccessfully – to disrupt the group.

The majority of discussion group participants appeared interested in and willing to help with the study, and pleased to be asked for their opinions. However, most were sceptical about the extent to which our report, or their views, would be taken on board by those in a position to make a difference. Responses to our questionnaire were in the main considered and thoughtful. Levels of tolerance between group members were generally high and it was interesting to hear the differing perceptions that individual group members brought to the discussion. The most vociferous group members were the young offenders.

In only two prisons did education staff sit in on the discussion. It is difficult to comment on the extent to which their presence influenced the discussion. In one of the groups, prisoner-learners clearly had a positive relationship with the member of staff and most were familiar with and confident at participating in a group discussion. The second smaller group of prisoners not in education were less forthcoming. This may well have been as a result of a member of staff being present.

4.   Outline of this report

The body of this report in part two will present the prisoners' perspective on education, in an order which roughly corresponds with the prisoners' own experience. Thus we begin with the process by which prisoners' educational needs are assessed and how they get access to education. We also consider issues such as incentives and pay. We then turn to the curriculum, discussing the prisoners' views on the range of courses available to them, the place of basic education and their ideas about what else is needed. Following this, we turn to the variety of previous experiences of education which prisoner-learners bring into prison with them. The next section will look at more general feedback on the place of prison education: its value for prisoners and the drawbacks they perceive. The prisoners' sense of how others view their education is surveyed next, including their impressions of the views and attitudes of education staff, prison officers, governors, probation officers, and family and friends. A final section looks forward, considering the relevance of prison education to resettlement and continued learning outside. Building upon the reported views of prisoners, we conclude with some ideas about how to encourage learning in prison, and then provide detailed recommendations for change.

THE VIEWS OF PRISONERS

1. Prison Life and The Prison Education Context

1.1 Induction and assessment

Going to prison is bound to be a dislocating and distressing experience. In the first few days educational needs are unlikely to be at the forefront of any prisoner's mind. Amongst the many orders, examinations and assessments to which prisoners will be subject, they may be asked to take a test to assess their educational abilities.

How are educational needs assessed in prison? There was some variation in the responses from the groups. It appeared that some prisons were running a standard basic skills test as a part of the induction process. In some of these, the assessments seemed to be working well:

> 'You do literacy and numeracy and then there's a dyslexia test so they can spot if you've got special needs.' (adult and YOI Cat B).

> 'I did an English and numeracy test – they grade you to see your level.'
> (C Cat Training – NIE)

But this was not the case everywhere. Some groups, particularly in local prisons, reported a lack of any educational assessment:

> 'I came in. There was no assessment. I was allocated to a certain job. On D wing you do teabags. On C wing you do wheelchairs.' (local)

> 'Some other prisons assess you. It doesn't seem to happen here.' (local)

> 'Other gaols do assessments as part of induction.' (local NIE)

> 'I think they should assess everyone when you start.' (local NIE)

In three prisons we heard that the same test was repeated everywhere:

> 'I've done exactly the same educational needs assessment half a dozen times in other prisons.' (C Cat training)

Some prisoners said that they had declined to take the test:

> 'I didn't do the test because I didn't want to. She tried her best to get me on it.' (Prisoner who has trouble reading, C Cat Training – NIE)

In his prison, there seemed no alternative ways of getting your learning needs met. But even where assessments were undertaken, there seemed to be a gap between low achievement and help with basic skills:

> 'I couldn't do the test. So they said they'd put me on education.'
> (adult and YOI B Cat NIE)

But he was still waiting, several months later.

Another prisoner, who had not gained a place on education, was anxious that he had been left out:

> 'I've been in two months. People coming down after me have gone down there [to the education department]. I'm dyslexic. I should be going down there before them.'
> (adult and YOI B Cat NIE)

1.2   Getting access to education

How do prisoners who want to pursue education get on courses?

We were told frequently by those in the NIE groups that they had tried to get to classes, but their applications had not borne fruit. Nor did they seem to know whether their application had ever been received by the education department, let alone actioned. There was simply no response. From the prisoners' perception, the process of dealing with their applications to attend classes was often unintelligible. The suspicion that unwanted applications were simply 'lost' in the system came through regularly from these groups.

A young prisoner expressed an unmet desire for education:

> 'I think everyone should go. They should be made to go. I've been stuck working on the wings for 13 months. I'd do history. I'd do anything.' (adult and YOI B cat NIE)

But for some reason his applications were not acted on.

It was striking how many prisoners not in education said they wanted to be 'on classes'. In five of the ten NIE groups, prisoners said they had been trying repeatedly, unsuccessfully, to get there. They did not know what had happened to their applications. In seven groups, respondents said they would like to do education, but either what they wanted to do was not available, or they weren't allowed to do it (e.g., Open University courses) or they would have to sacrifice too much (gym, their job, pay) to go. Even those who hadn't tried to get on classes thought they should:

> 'I ain't done it. But really and truly I know education is the key. All the successful people are well educated.' (local NIE)

Right from the start of our discussions, the need and desire for more opportunities for learning were expressed convincingly.

We heard frequently that getting onto classes seemed to depend more on luck, or influence, than judgement.

> 'I got onto education completely accidentally. I'm a white guy and I found myself on a black drama group. They mixed up the names. But once I got down here, I could get on the classes I wanted.' (local)

The influence of staff was significant:

> 'If [the administrator is] not here, it's down to luck. X is for the inmates.' (local)

Knowing the education orderly (prisoner assistant in the education department) was also a help, as was a spell in the hospital:

> 'I was in the hospital wing. I did a couple of drawings and they said, "Right, you're on." Staff put out feelers and you're on.' (local)

Prisoners in local prisons, in particular, seemed to feel that access to educational opportunity was a hit-and-miss affair, that favouritism might be a factor, and that it was a matter of who you knew, or who was on duty. The sense of a reliable application procedure, with an understandable system of priorities, was lacking.

Waiting lists seemed to be a problem everywhere. Predictably, the popular classes, like cooking and computers, often had waiting lists.

> 'Everything has waiting lists but cookery has the longest waiting lists – 70 people. It's a joke. I waited three months, then the teacher was on holiday, then she dropped something on her foot and was off sick. That's another three months.' (YOI)

Other NIE respondents said there was a waiting list just to get on education:

> 'It was offered in November, but it's March and I'm still waiting.' (local, NIE)

> 'Only every now and then do you see vacancies on the labour board saying there are places on education.' (dispersal)

Nearly all the groups criticised the limitations on budgets and space for education, which meant that few prisoners could benefit. We were also told regularly that the education department did not advertise its classes: there was no published programme, or regular information about what classes were running. Given the waiting lists for popular classes, perhaps this was unsurprising. However this was another way in which prison education departed from common practice in the community.

1.3   Personal choice

To what extent were prisoners free to decide what they wanted to study?

Most prisoners, especially those in the longer-term gaols, felt their personal choice of courses and classes was limited, not only in terms of what was on offer, and their chances of getting to classes, but also by what the prison would or would not allow.

> 'First they see how long you're doing, whether you're a lifer etc. Then they look at your offence, and what character you are. Then they... The short version is, the prison decides!' (dispersal)

Access to Open University courses appeared to be strictly limited. Prisoners in the dispersal prisons particularly resented this, and the extent to which eligibility was determined by your category, sentence length, and regime status. (In one prison, we were told that only those on an enhanced regime could apply.) We discuss this further below.

Whilst most who wanted to (though not all, especially in the local prisons) could come to basic skills classes, there were problems for those wanting to do some manual skills training courses, as well as the higher-level academic options, on security grounds.

> 'If you're in for stabbing that rules you out of cookery, where you've got knives. And motor mechs, and P and D [painting and decorating]. It's one of the things they'll look at.' (YOI)

1.4   Sentence planning

Was education included in sentence planning?

There was a wide disparity of views. People who had been in longer on the same sentence seemed more likely to have a sentence plan, but still there were puzzling discrepancies. The first question was whether the prisoners had a sentence plan or not. The second was whether educational needs were included in the sentence plan.

In most of the local prisons, groups said they did not have sentence plans.

> *'What sentence plan?'* (adult and YOI Cat B NIE)

There was often a sense of grievance that sentence plans had not been completed, or reviewed:

> *'My last gaol, I was there nine months and not one of them was done. That's what makes the inmate go back to his cell and kick off.'* (YOI)

The general impression from the groups was that even where sentence planning was done, education rarely featured. Prisoner-learners felt that staff considered education an occasional add-on, rather than a core aspect of sentence planning. As prisoners saw it, offending behaviour programmes took priority:

> *'To be truthful, it seems they want you to do the courses that look good for them other than education, like ETS [Enhanced Thinking Skills]. And it's not that people want to do them; they have to. It's part of their SP [sentence plan].'* (dispersal)

> *'I have a sentence plan. Education is not on it. ETS is on it. ETS has a 600 people waiting list. I've got to meet targets by a certain date. Do I get priority?'* (local NIE)

Only a few prisoners described a sentence plan that included education. Other respondents certainly thought it should:

> *'Education should be on the sentence plan for some people, if they can't read or write.'* (C Cat training – NIE)

Another long-term prisoner commented:

> *'After a few years they run out of things to say. So it's just, "Carry on with education." It's not really a plan.'* (dispersal)

In contrast, some of the groups also described encouragement coming through less formal routes:

> *'I was called into the office – the probation officer, my personal officer and someone else – all they said was, "You can carry on going to the gym and the workshop," and recommended that I did some education.'* (dispersal NIE)

This group member went on to say:

> *'I done a test and that was it. I was offered some classes but it didn't fit in with the gym and I'm happy with what I'm doing now.'* (dispersal NIE)

Another prisoner spoke of a more coercive type of encouragement:

> *'A number of guys have been told, "You're going on education or you're going UB40."'* (dispersal, NIE)

The impression we were left with was that sentence planning was uneven and that where it happened, education and training were not considered a core element. Most prisoners in these discussions appeared to accept, in principle, the idea of sentence planning. However there was little sense that they felt themselves to be joint negotiators in these target-setting exercises. Sentence plans seemed to be yet another thing that was done to them, rather than with them.

1.5 Pay

How did prisoners feel about rates of pay for education?

Pay was certainly a topic of concern, in every group, once we had raised it.   Once again, there was no consistent pattern across the prisons in our study. For example, it appeared that some prisons offered educational bonuses; others did not:

> 'You get £2.50 for passing exams.' (YOI)

The irony in being paid to receive education did not escape some. Several prisoners recognised that, on the outside, they would have to pay for it themselves:

> 'My girlfriend's doing Spanish and it costs her. She tells me at least I'm getting it for free.' (dispersal)

For the majority, however, it seemed there were better paying opportunities to be found, as this exchange from an adult and YOI B category prison (NIE group) makes clear. When asked whether anything put them off going to education they said:

> 'The pay. It's £6-9 here.'

> 'Industries is £15-20 a week.'

> 'I was working on the hospital wing. I was used to £15 a week.'

For prisoners with limited private cash, this was hard. It meant that prisoner-learners were significantly worse off when it came to buying toiletries, phone cards, or tobacco. It was harder still for particular minority groups, as a woman pointed out:

> 'A lot of us are foreign nationals. If you want to call home it costs £9 to talk to your relatives for half an hour.' (closed prison)

Poor pay for coming to classes was a serious disincentive for many. And there seemed no other way to get those educational needs met – or none that we heard about.

But in some prisons, however, the differential between pay for work and education was not significant, unless you worked in one of the contract workshops. According to the respondents, the contract workshops were, in many prisons, both better paid, and desperate for workers. But at least one prisoner expressed an objection to this policy:

> 'People are just stuck in workshops and not really asked if they want any help. Instead of just allocating people to an activity, you should match people to their level and to their need.' (Local NIE)

The workshops were the big payers. However, as one group member noted, if they did not pay so well they would be empty. The work was tedious, on the whole. Further, work did not seem readily available in all prisons we visited, and there was some frustration amongst those waiting in their cells, unemployed.

When we asked those in the NIE groups what put them off going to classes, low pay got six mentions, whilst lack of access to gym got eight.

There was a view that the pay was irrelevant:

> 'A lot of inmates would do education for nothing. It's not about the money. We said, "We don't do LTS [Learning Through Sport] for money. We'll just do it."' (local NIE)

There must be a better way to factor in the educational component, so that this false link with pay could be broken. If education attracts low pay in some prisons, what messages does this give out to prisoners about its value?

1.6   A right or a privilege?

The principle that prisoners are entitled to the same quality of education as they could access outside suggests that education in prison is a right. In practice, it seems that, given the demand for places, education is often treated as a privilege. The notion that prisoners might be punished by the withdrawal or withholding of education undermines the use of time in prison for rehabilitative aims. But although no one actually said they had been taken off education as punishment, we heard that prisoners, or others they knew, had been taken off classes for disruptive behaviour:

> 'I got kicked off my other English class. I was asking her how to spell a word and she wouldn't tell me. She kicked me out and said I was bad.' (YOI)

One young offender spoke of penalties for non-attendance:

> 'The thing I don't like is, if you don't feel like going [to classes] in this prison you get nicked. You might just feel depressed. You might have had a confrontation with your officer, or a phone call with your Mum. You might just want to rest on your bed. But you've got to go.' (YOI)

Another spoke of officers in his previous prison, who had adopted a punitive attitude to the whole enterprise:

> 'In HMP X, the POs said, "If they [the prisoners] do education we'll make them do it instead of exercise".' (YOI)

Halfway into the series of visits, we started to ask prisoners explicitly whether they regarded education in prison as a right or a privilege. There was a mixture of views. The majority, where asked, thought education was a right.

> 'If a prisoner wants to improve his education he should have a right.' (adult and YOI C Cat)

Another noted:

> 'They have race relations officers, anti-bullying officers. We need education officers, to champion it.' (local).

The 'privilege' part of the question switched many straight in to the mindset cultivated by the Incentives and Earned Privileges (IEP) scheme. The scheme was introduced several years ago to help manage behaviour in prison. Three separate regimes exist: basic, standard and enhanced.

It appeared that IEP status was being used to restrict educational opportunities, particularly in the long-stay prisons. In one prison, we were told you could not do some things like degree level work unless you were on enhanced status – the highest level. And it seemed you would not get this privilege unless you took part in offending behaviour groups.

> *'I was prevented from doing a law course here. You have to be on enhanced status. They're making it tricky. To get on enhanced status you have to go on groups. The governor says you've got to. I asked to pay for my course myself but [the education manager] says I can't.'* (dispersal)

The impact of earned incentives on all aspects of prison life was, where it occurred, much resented. Just as strongly resented was the involvement of education staff with prison discipline – though we only heard of a couple of instances where this happened.

Sometimes, where there were not many options for purposeful activity during the day, education appeared to be the dumping ground for those who had not applied for jobs. Governors have had targets for hours spent out of cell on 'purposeful activity' for longer than they have had education targets to meet:

> *'In this prison, education is not a privilege. If you don't apply for work, you'll get put on education.'* (adult male and YOI B Cat)

The right to choose did not seem to feature here. But when asked for their impressions of what prison staff thought, the boot was on the other foot. Without exception, where asked, respondents thought prison staff saw education for prisoners as a privilege:

> *'Here the prison officers will tell you it's a privilege.'* (local)

> *'They want to keep education small. Exams cost a lot. They're always moaning about the budget.'* (local)

The message seemed to be that these were scarce resources, for non-essentials, to be distributed parsimoniously. Education meant exams, and these were expensive. In this prison, it did not sound as though education was seen as a vital part of the reform and resettlement agenda for inmates – at least from a prisoner's perspective.

1.7   The prison timetable

Far more significant than pay, for some, were the other sacrifices called for if you came to classes. Gym was universally a casualty. But in one prison it was worse than that:

> *'If you're on education you miss out on everything: exercise, showers, phone calls, kit change. You sacrifice a lot.'* (local)

> *'You can have showers at the weekend, but there's no hot water. Everyone wants one.'* (local)

> *'You know who's on education: they smell!'* (local)

In more than one prison we heard vigorous complaints about the shortage of time in the mornings:

> *'Disgraceful. They open us up at 8.05 and we have to do everything by 8.30. It's ridiculous.'* (dispersal)

> *'Education starts at 8 here. We need clocks in our cells so people can be ready.'* (local)

When shortage of time combined with negative attitudes towards education on the part of officers, the results could be explosive:

> *'I was brushing my teeth when the officer unlocked me. I said, "Just one second governor," and he said, "No," and slammed the door. I flipped.'* (local)

1.8   Security categories and their knock-on effects

The longer-term prisoners found the restrictions and (in their eyes) the lack of logic, in hampering their access to these and similar educational opportunities, irksome:

> *'They've got a plastering course but because I'm Cat A I can't do it. There's guys on the plasterers that won't be out for 20 years. I'm Cat A but I'll be out in two years. That's the only useful thing I could do here that'd give me a job on release. I could leave prison a bricklayer, plasterer and plumber. I've done plumbing at HMP X.'* (dispersal)

As one member of our advisory group put it:

> *'We know that there are likely to be other factors that brought about this comment. But this quote encapsulates...the lack of communication between the two groups, the consumers and the providers.'*

2.   The Curriculum

2.1   What courses were available in the prisons visited?

We asked everyone in our study what education they were doing, in their current prison, and what they had studied previously, either as part of this or earlier sentences. The variety of responses indicated the range of what was on offer, across the prison estate. In terms of class-based learning we heard about:

Table Three: Prisoners' list of subjects available to them

Basic and key skills	English, maths and IT at levels 1,2,3
Social and life skills	Cooking, woodwork, home maintenance, health and social care, citizenship, personal development, budgeting, sign language, first aid, welfare to work, assertiveness, parentcraft, child development, listening (run through Samaritans)
Academic courses	Open University degree courses, A and AS level philosophy and English literature, GCSE courses in English and maths, psychology, sociology, history. GNVQ art and design, French, German, Spanish, geography, media studies
Creative and recreative classes	art, music, pottery, camera studies, drama, yoga, Shakespeare drama workshops, creative writing
Business and IT training	GNVQ Business Studies, RSA, CLAIT, ECDL (European Computer Driving Licence) in computing, Firm Start (business start-up), Going Solo (self employment), business administration
Vocational skills training	plastering, bricklaying, catering, braille, fashion design, food prep and hygiene, joinery, motor mechanics, horticulture, sports and leisure, teaching gym, Learning through Sport, Community Sports Leaders Award, hairdressing and beauty, computer aided design (CAD), technical drawing, welding, electrical wiring, City and Guilds shoemaking

Some of these courses were certificated and some were not. The majority were run by the education department: others were undertaken in the vocational training workshops, through the chapel, or through charities. The prisoners did not always differentiate.

Sometimes prisoner-learners told us, under this heading, about courses which sounded like Offending Behaviour Programmes, run by psychology or probation departments: CARAT (Counselling, Assessment, Referral, Advice, Throughcare), ETS (Enhanced Thinking Skills), R and R (Reasoning and Rehabilitation), anger management, drug and alcohol awareness. What is within the education manager and the contractor's remit sometimes appeared arbitrary. To the prisoners, there didn't seem much difference: they listed these as 'courses' and so they were.

2.2   The variability of provision in different types of establishment

The table below shows prisoner-learners' perceptions of what was on offer in five of the prisons in the study. There were differences between similar types of prison, as well as between prisons in different categories. The table shows both the rich mix of subjects available, and also some of the discontinuity.

Table Four: Prisoners' lists of courses available by type of prison

	archaeology (private study)	art	assertive-ness	budgeting	business	camera studies	carpentry	catering & food preparation	citizenship	computing	cooking	drama
Local		Yes			Yes	Yes				Yes		
Training		Yes		Yes	Yes		Yes		Yes	Yes	Yes	
YOI		Yes	Yes					Yes		Yes	Yes	Yes
Women					Yes			Yes		Yes		
Dispersal	Yes									Yes		

	English	French	general studies	geography	German	Going Solo	hairdressing and beauty	health & social care	home maintenance	key skills	life and social skills	maths
Local	Yes									Yes		Yes
Training	Yes					Yes		Yes		Yes		Yes
YOI	Yes									Yes		Yes
Women	Yes						Yes		Yes	Yes	Yes	Yes
Dispersal	Yes	Yes	Yes	Yes	Yes							Yes

	Open learning	Open University	parenting	personal development	pottery	psychology	resettlement	Shakespeare drama workshops	sociology	Spanish	typing
Local							Yes	Yes			Yes
Training			Yes	Yes	Yes	Yes			Yes		
YOI		Yes									
Women											
Dispersal	Yes	Yes								Yes	

Local prisons

There were certainly some anomalies, with the short-stay big locals apparently the most versatile in what they offered. Short, roll-on roll-off courses, with an emphasis on basic skills, recreational and creative subjects, were commonplace.

Training prisons

Within the prisons in our survey there were marked inconsistencies, even within the same categories, in what was on offer.

The sparsest curriculum, appeared to be at one of the cat C training prisons.

> 'There's no pottery here, no art, nothing. Just English, maths and computers.'

Another had the most varied curriculum of any of the prisons we visited. There may well have been good reasons for this difference, but the contrast between prisoners' perceptions of the two programmes was marked.

Long-term prisons

The dispersal prisons offered more of an academic curriculum, which was clearly geared to the needs of prisoners who would be staying a while.

Both long-stay prisons offered open learning schemes. This involved prisoner-learners coming down to the education wing and working on their own with some tutorial support. We also heard of 'flexi' which sounded like the same sort of thing, in a number of establishments.

Women's prisons

In both women's prisons there seemed to be a focus on vocational courses and life skills. There was no discernible academic curriculum, as far as group members reported it.

One prisoner-learner remarked:

> *'Other prisons offer basic maths, English, craft skills: most offer the same range of courses. A nice range of useless things.'* (women's prison)

In the women's prisons we visited arts and crafts was the subject most missed, and particularly sewing.

> *'There are not even machines here. At [HMP X] they had a tailoring department. We made clothes for third world countries.'* (women's prison)

We asked both groups in the two women's prisons whether there were classes that particularly supported the needs of women. A discussion of this topic revealed some varied opinions.

The closed women's prison had re-roled from male to female within the previous eighteen months to address the escalating numbers within the women's estate. One woman thought this still showed in the curriculum:

> *'In HMP X and HMP Y they had domestic violence and hygiene [classes] which taught about sexually transmitted diseases and other classes specifically focused on women. Here we're still a male prison. They still address us with the attitude as for a mister.'* (women's prison)

When a fellow group member noted that there were 'quite a few leaflets in the health centre', the same respondent replied:

> *'They're very good at having leaflets, but what's the point if people have a problem reading?'* (women's prison)

The same cluster of topics came up in the open women's prison. A desire for more on 'personal health' was expressed, with an emphasis on drug and alcohol awareness and healthy eating.

Young Offenders

Although we visited three prisons in which adult and young offenders were both held, we only visited one prison exclusively for 18-21 year olds.

A young man on the parenting course in this prison felt very positive about the course:

> *'We get opportunities to write books for our kids. It's good. What a woman feels going through labour. You learn things. You know some different stuff for next time, when she's worrying about it.'* (YOI)

We heard a lot about the cookery course, which was the one with the longest waiting list. We also heard about the trade courses, run in the workshops. The motor mechanics course was particularly popular. But many were irritated by the shortage of places:

> *'Problem is, if they had more things for us to do, we could spread out. There's 12 spaces in motor mechs and 350 people. There's not enough spaces, and not enough courses for us to do.'* (YOI)

For some, education seemed to be the place where prisoners had to mark time until the things they really wanted to do became available:

> 'They're telling me if I want to get onto a [trade] course I've got to wait. But meanwhile I've got to do something I don't want to do. I want to do P and D [painting and decorating]. But I've got to do education. If I don't I'll get nicked.' (YOI)

Learning Opportunities for Black and Minority Ethnic Prisoners

Black and Minority Ethnic (BME) prisoners were over-represented in our sample, by three per cent, relative to their numbers in the prison population. This may have something to do with their generally higher levels of educational attainment on their arrival in prison, and/or their positive attitude towards using whatever educational opportunities the prison offered.

Women prisoners were over-represented too, because we wanted to visit both a closed and an open prison. However, unlike women and young prisoners, BME prisoners are not treated separately in the Prison Service structure. Therefore we did not speak to any BME group in isolation: all of the groups were racially mixed.

We asked all groups whether there were any classes specifically addressing the needs of black and minority ethnic prisoners.

There seemed to be some initial awkwardness about tackling this question in the majority of our groups, compared, for instance, to questions about prison staff. But where people were prepared to talk openly, discussions focused around the teaching of, and resources for, independent learning about black history.

In one third of the sample it appeared that the prison did offer some classroom work, though it was not always appreciated:

> 'You don't get any qualifications off Black History so it's pointless.' (C Cat training)

In the majority of groups in prisons where such classes or courses did not seem to be offered, opinions were divided as to their value.   Some were against, thinking 'they should treat everyone the same.' However the majority, in our racially mixed groups, were in favour:

> 'Nothing here. We can learn about the British Empire...' (dispersal)

> 'I reckon there should be. Everyone wants to know their history.' (C Cat adult and YOI)

However the more general point concerned a dearth of resources for self-study:

> 'They should have black history books in the library because a lot of kids are mixed race. I could learn about their history and tell them.' (women's prison)

2.3   The core curriculum

In most groups there was a recognition that the focus of prison education had shifted over the past few years away from the eclectic and individual programmes of previous years towards literacy, numeracy and IT.

Literacy

Although many lamented the demise – or at least the dramatic decline – of evening classes, and the shortage of funding for academic, vocational and creative subjects, there was an endorsement in 90 per cent of the groups, whether attending classes or not, of the vital importance of decent literacy skills.

> 'A lot of inmates who haven't got reading and writing make up for their inadequacies in other ways like going out thieving. They should be given the abilities to read and write.' (dispersal NIE)

The same man went on to speak about the pleasures of reading, and his sense that the non-readers were being denied a valuable life-line in prison:

> 'Then look at the library and the enjoyment you can get there. When I read a good book I can picture the scenarios. It's a shame that other people haven't got those needs met.' (dispersal – NIE)

Another NIE prisoner in a large local prison knew it made sense to go, but had got fed up with waiting for his applications to bear fruit.

> 'Best thing to do in here. My Mum says I should go, cos my reading's not too clever, but it takes too long to get over there.'

He had taken a workshop job. Another in the same group was clear about his special educational needs, from school days:

> 'The teacher would write on the board. I used to get half way through it and she'd wipe it off. I used to get upset.'

He said he had put in 'so many applications' for classes, but had so far been unsuccessful.

Despite the importance attached to basic skills in prison education, group members felt that the needs of significant numbers of people who could not read and write were still not being met. In one third of the sample of prisons, respondents said that either they, or others they knew, had lacked the support or the opportunity to get to classes, even though their literacy deficits were clear. This could be for a number of reasons: the main ones mentioned were lack of adequate provision on the prison's part, and a need to save face, on the individual's:

> 'There's a lot of people who have hardly any literacy skills but they're too proud or shy to come up with it.' (local)

Another group member, in another prison, who wanted 'more opportunities for people who struggle academically,' spoke of...

> 'a 23 or 24 year old kid who is motivated enough but can hardly read or write. Workshops are not releasing people because they are down on their numbers. Education should be given a higher priority..... That kid [who was turned down for education] will probably not ask anyone else again.' (local)

In another local, the group perception was that 'people with literacy problems aren't seen much down here.' In this group, members believed that doing badly in the induction test would mean you did not get on to classes – or at least that the less well you did, the longer it would take.

Help for people with dyslexia

Fairly consistently, the groups were aware of dyslexia, knew that it was a condition that could be effectively managed, and saw the potential for special programmes to benefit people with the condition. Assessment for dyslexia was mentioned in some, but not in all of the discussions, and specialist help, including interactive computer programmes, was mentioned. A number of respondents spoke with something like relief about the feeling that they had, at last, had their special educational needs recognised, and met:

> 'The help with dyslexia has made me feel I am somebody, that I can do something. In school I was drifting.' (local)

Speakers of other languages

There was a fair degree of concern for people in prison who couldn't speak English, as this series of contributions from one of the women's prisons shows:

> 'They don't get attention because they're not understood.'

> 'For some non-English speakers, the European languages staff probably understand. But for Albanians, Kosovans, Afghans there's not enough.'

> 'There is a Kosovan lady who didn't get any attention apart from one other fellow inmate – she is crying – she needs proper interpretation. She's still here long after her sentence.' (women's prison)

Maths

There was much less overt enthusiasm for maths. An interchange from one of our dispersal groups is typical:

> 'I hate that subject.'

> 'Yeah, but it's generally been a help.'

> 'Maths is generally what people don't want to do.'

> 'You quite need it though. You just do it.' (dispersal)

One man, who acknowledged he needed help with both maths and English, said frankly:

> 'On the out, I'm struggling measuring up for concrete.' (local)

IT, computing and business skills

Computer skills were prized. In every prison we visited, the IT provision was well used and much valued. In over half, both the equipment and teaching were highly regarded. And, although there was some doubt as to whether they would be able to raise loans to get started, courses teaching business skills for self-employment were also particularly valued.

But there was room for improvement. In half of the groups, prisoner-learners regarded both hardware and software as 'old and outdated'.

> 'Oh God, sometimes you have to sit there five minutes just to get the programme started. We need more advanced stuff.' (women's prison)

However it wasn't like this everywhere. In some groups respondents acknowledged that 'they've got excellent equipment' (C Cat Training).

Lack of internet access was particularly bemoaned amongst those doing higher level work:

> 'All we need is ten minutes supervised access to complete assignments (for the Open University). I can't do any of the web-based designs.' (dispersal)

It is difficult to believe that the obvious risks and temptations associated with unfettered access to the internet could not be overcome with a little imagination, computer know-how and institutional courage.

In one local prison, the praise for both the equipment and the teaching was particularly warm:

> 'There's a very helpful teacher. He pushes you and pushes you.'

> 'They've got Pentium 2/3 processors: good equipment, a scanner and a printer.'

> 'All I knew before was spreadsheets and data-processing. I learned a lot here. You can do web-designing.' (local)

We were struck by the variety of provision across the system, the vagaries of the curriculum and the variability of the equipment. It really seemed very much the luck of the draw whether you got a good IT learning experience or not – although the same could be said of many schools and colleges in the wider community.

2.4   The broader curriculum

Vocational training

Skills-based and accredited training for work, where it existed, was valued highly. In all but two of the 22 groups, whether attending classes or not, prisoners asked for more manual skills and trade courses. The lack of capacity in workshops was widely lamented.

> 'They do have bricklaying and a carpentry course here, but there's a six month waiting list. You have to be doing four years to get on.' (adult and YOI C Cat)

In prison, vocational skills training has traditionally not been run by education departments. This is another way in which the disjuncture between education in prison and education in the community shows up. In most colleges of further education (and most of the contractors providing education in prisons are FE colleges), these activities go on side by side. However we understand this is soon to change.

The creative arts

Where there were art, pottery, drama, music and similar classes available, these were very much valued. As has been recognised for some time, such opportunities can uncover hidden talents and provide a route into education for people for whom school had been a negative experience. For one woman, unable to read or write when she came into prison, art classes had done wonders for her self-esteem:

> 'I want to do art college [on release]. I didn't think I could draw. I came to prison and I realised that I can draw. I used to think, "Look at those hippies going to college" – and I can draw!' (women's open)

She had also astonished herself by gaining some GCSEs, along the way.

Self-expression was perceived in one in four of the prisoner-learner groups as of therapeutic value: such classes provided a much-needed safety valve.

'The art tutor got me to express my anger on paper: calmed me down.' (local)

'Art – it's for everyone isn't it? Not whether you are good or not. You can express yourself. If you're having a hard time something like that helps.' (Adult and YOI C Cat – NIE)

Some voiced their sense that arts could be considered subversive:

'The governors want to stop pottery etc. But getting rid of creativity is getting rid of free thinking.' (local)

Music was the course most desired, and least provided. Prisoners praised the music courses they had had at other prisons, and longed to have another chance.

Drama was also mentioned by two individuals as something they enjoyed, or would enjoy. As one said:

'Life's a great big stage and I don't feel I've been acting too well.' (dispersal)

2.5   Continuity

Was there continuity in education which meant that prisoners who were transferred from one prison to another could expect to continue their courses?

The groups responded in different ways to this question. In one local there was a faith in logic and computers:

'At the other prison they'll ask and try to put you back on the same level.' (local)

And in another, there was consensus that it wouldn't be too hard:

'If you leave this prison and you're doing a qualification that's not offered in another prison you can go outside [to college] or you can transfer to a gaol that offers that course.' (local)

As regards the transfer of records, again, some local groups seemed to have had good experiences:

'My certificates came through and they chased my GCSE certificates from school.' (local)

Two prisoners mentioned the use of discs for the transport of work between prisons. Others doing exam courses took their own work with them in hard copy format:

'I've got my paperwork in a folder.' (YOI AS student)

However, the experience of those who had been in the system longer was not so good. When asked what happened when he'd moved prisons, one young prisoner-learner remarked succinctly:

'Nothing. The course stops. End of.' (YOI)

In some cases, there were serious consequences:

'I moved prison when I was only one month away from doing exams, A levels, and I couldn't do the exams. They wouldn't release my work.' (Dispersal)

In over half the groups, we heard that efforts to retrieve work and certificates from the previous prison, despite efforts by staff in the current gaol, had proved fruitless:

'There's been a few occasions when X tried to chase up stuff from HMP X. I was rushed here so quickly I didn't have a chance to pick anything up from the Education Department. They rang up several times but it didn't come through.' (Cat C Training)

> 'Any prison you go in, you wait two to three months for your papers. They don't come. You start at the beginning again.' (dispersal)

> 'When I told them what I'd done in HMP X it was like, "Well, your papers haven't come through, so how do we know?"' (women's prison)

This delay/non-arrival/disappearance of records was a constant complaint. As two prisoners noted:

> 'You don't have an education file that follows you.' (dispersal)

> 'You wouldn't think it would be that difficult.' (adult/YOI C cat)

Reading between the lines, pressures to meet basic skills targets appeared to loom large, to judge by responses in a number of the groups.

> 'I had to retake some exams just to prove I could do them. I have two copies of the certificate, one from HMP X and one from HMP Y.' (C Cat Training)

> 'If you're doing education and you get English and maths levels one and two and once you pass you get chucked back in your cell.' (Adult and YOI C Cat)

The introduction of some kind of learning passport, which a prisoner could easily take with them on transfer, would seem a step forward.

But in some cases, it was hard to tell whether respondents had been put on classes for their own needs, or just to bump up the numbers:

> 'They said, "Would you like to do the basic skills?" I said I'd already done them. I want to learn what I want to learn. But you haven't got a choice.' (Dispersal)

And in one local, in the not in education group, one prisoner had been asked to sit an exam without having been anywhere near the classes.

> 'I failed it. I'm sure I'd have passed it if I'd even gone to a couple of classes to get the techniques.' (local – NIE)

Clearly the opportunities to do other things had been curtailed, as prisoners saw it, to make room for the basic skills classes. When asked whether the prison considered some classes as more important than others, two contributors in one of our dispersal prison groups commented:

> 'Basic Skills has been pushed: quite a few things have been dropped.' (dispersal)

> 'Level one and two classes were seen as more important than others. If you're above a certain level, there are a few people who have real problems.' (dispersal)

The pressure to meet targets could work against the least able, some felt – presumably because they were not able to help deliver the necessary numbers of passes at levels one and two. Referring to the deputy education manager, one prisoner remarked:

> 'X is only doing his job. He's got to get his KPTs. I didn't have a problem, but the basic people get left out.' (local)

There was a fair degree of consensus about priorities, however. Even the most ambitious recognised that the needs of the least able should be met first. And one man, for whom prison education had clearly done a lot, said simply:

> 'I can read. That changes the way you think about things. You can approach things in the right way.' (local)

2.6   Formal and informal opportunities: learning elsewhere in the prison

Distance learning and private study

The Open University was the most regularly mentioned distance-learning provider, followed by the National Extension College. Often the Prisoners' Education Trust was mentioned, as a funder of art materials and correspondence courses. The prisoner-learner's life was often made more difficult, however, by prison restrictions about what they could keep in their cells.

> 'I'm doing GCSE maths by myself and an OU course in environmental studies – it's possible to do these with a long sentence. But prison has stupid rules: you're not allowed a scientific calculator in the cells.' (women's prison)

The Open University degree courses were much prized. For many in the long-stay prisons, variability of access to OU studies was one of the most keenly felt injustices in the system. There was a passion for degrees.

In one of the cat C training prisons, a flexible package was possible:

> 'Self-study (OU) where my time's split between cell and the library and I come to some classes, and sociology.' (C Cat training)

This sort of flexibility was rare. We heard much more about what wasn't allowed, than what was.

Use of the library

One prisoner-learner, a library orderly, mentioned 'self study in the library' (dispersal). This prison had a lovely library, visible from the room in which we held our discussion. However we did not see anybody using it while we were there. This may have been in order not to disturb our group, because of staff sickness, or some other reason. However it seemed significant in the context of our question to all group members about access to the library.

In five prisons, group members thought the library was good, or even excellent. Not only the range of stock, but also the service librarians were able to provide for individual prisoners, were the key to their star ratings:

> 'You can read in there. Get CDs and cassettes. Very interesting, the library.' (women's prison)

> 'The library's brilliant. They'll order anything you want. I've ordered books that only two libraries have and they've got them for me.' (dispersal NIE)

Sometimes the librarian, and the individual attention and service provided, seemed to be the most highly valued aspects.

> 'The librarian is excellent. I've enormous respect for her.'

> 'It used to be a joke but she's turned it round.' (dispersal)

Lack of access was the main bugbear, however. For some, being on education was a key to access, in that the library was actually located within the education block:

> 'In HMP X it was impossible to get any books to help you. Here, the library's right there.' (adult and YOI B Cat)

> 'If you're doing history you can go and get a book to help you.' (adult and YOI B Cat)

> 'You can go once a week and that's it. But if you're here, you can go if you have a pass.' (YOI)

But for the majority, however good the library was, the main problem was getting there:

> 'For the YOs, they only let about 15 over every week.' (adult and YOI B Cat)

> 'Twelve people a week get to go to the library. There's 90 on the wing. Everyone should have a chance. The library's good.' (adult and YOI B Cat – NIE)

One group member highlighted the problem of returning or renewing books, where access was limited:

> 'At the end of the wing there's a box. It's meant to take books back but they don't. Now I can't take books out of the library.' (local)

In one in three of our groups, where access to the library was not directly from the education department, prisoners seemed to be forced to choose between classes or getting access to the library, at least on weekdays.

> 'Education finishes at 11.30 and the library closes at 11.45. Sometimes the gate [to leave the education block] isn't even open by then.' (women's prison)

This was particularly acute in one local:

> 'I've never got to the library in six weeks from putting an application in. I'd never have got there at all, if it wasn't for [the basic skills tutor]. She will make sure. She'll bring you to the library.' (local)

In the same group, another member remarked:

> 'Books are harder to get than drugs in here. I could go to certain wings and pick up heroin any time. But not a book.' (local)

In-cell learning

Some prisoners described instances of learning in their cells:

> 'They give me home work.' (local)

> 'I'm writing a book on Treblinka.' (local)

One prisoner spoke with pride and satisfaction about the coursework for a sports course he had particularly enjoyed:

> 'The homework gives us something to do behind the doors. ... It keeps you occupied day and night. I was sat there a good three hours working on one assignment.' (local NIE)

Much seemed to depend on which officers were on duty:

> 'You can get opportunities (e.g., oil paints and art materials). But at the whim of an officer.' (local)

> 'You can work in your cell depending which officers are on.' (adult and YOI B cat)

And another remarked that access to educational opportunities, in this prison, could depend which wing you were on. The view that the regime and culture could differ significantly within the same establishment, depending on your wing, was apparent in three groups (one in four of our sample).

Puzzlingly, in one of the long stay prisons we were told without further explanation:

> *'This place doesn't allow people to work in their cells because they can't get the money.'* **(dispersal)**

However it wasn't like this everywhere.

> *'Desk, paints – I've got it all in my cell.'* **(Adult and YOI B Cat)**

> *'If you ask them they'll give it to you.'*

Of course much depended on whether you were on your own, or sharing. Sometimes your 'pad mate' could make things difficult, as this interchange from one of the local prison groups indicates:

> *'They're all two-man cells, so there's another man listening to the TV or radio. It's difficult to concentrate.'*

> *'I've got a nice cell-mate. He helps me.'*

> *'It's difficult to get a good cell-mate. I've got one who scribbles on my work.'* **(local)**

We heard a great deal, both positive and negative, about the impact of in-cell TV.

> *'Cell TV: it's a problem. My cellmate wants to watch programmes all night. I want the TV off at 12. I have to get up at seven to come down here.'* **(local)**

We also heard about the desire for more access to computers in cells. Laptops were not allowed, from what we heard, in any of these prisons, although in one of the dispersal prisons we were told you could have a 'typewriter with a memory'.

One particular drawback to using a prison sentence as an opportunity to study was brought home by a long-term prisoner in one of the dispersal prisons, who commented on the restrictions of volumetric control. Prisoners are allowed only a limited number of personal possessions, based on what can be stored in standard-sized cardboard boxes: one for prisoners serving short sentences, two for those with longer sentences:

> *'I have a box filled up with books. I'm only allowed two boxes to put personal stuff in. All my education stuff is taking up one box, so I've only got one box for the rest.'* **(dispersal)**

We also heard about the difficulties for prisoner-learners caused by cell-searches (when individuals' cells are searched for drugs and other prohibited things).

> *'If they turn us over they have to go through all the paperwork you've got.'* **(local)**

Peer learning

In two prisons we heard about prisoners learning to help others with their literacy skills: Peers Partners and Toe by Toe were schemes training prisoners to help others on the wings.

> *'Peers partners: assisting people with one to one literacy skills. It helps anyone with literacy or numeracy problems. They use the TV room for that. If you can't read or write or spell you need it.'* **(Adult and YOI B Cat)**

Where this was available, it was much appreciated. In one of the long-term gaols, however, it had been vetoed:

> *'I was learning to assist [people to read and write] at HMP X. I'd got nearly to the end. But I was told they don't do it here because it would give inmates power over other inmates.'* (dispersal)

In others, peer learning went on, but informally.

> *'On Monday I help out with adult literacy, EFL.'* (women's prison)

But another noted that 'helping other inmates isn't structured': there was no training for peer support it seemed.

Sport and gym

In four prisons we heard about courses run through the gym.

> *'... not just sports but physiology and science as well.'* (local)

Access, or lack of access, to the gym was one of the most frequent talking points. Access to the gym was highly prized, in all the prisons we visited:

> *'Gym comes before everything in gaol. You get a feeling of good spirits afterwards.'* (adult and YOI C Cat)

In some cases, access to gym was ruled out altogether if you did education. Maybe this was because the gym was fully occupied in working hours.

> *'During the week they're running courses in the gym – so it makes it difficult for others to do gym. But they're not run by education.'* (Adult male and YOI C Cat)

Sports related courses were very popular. One particular course, in a male local, which was run by people from the local university, was threatened with closure.

> *'Learning through sport – the course was extended to two days a week. It includes OCR level two English. They're trying to close the course. We were doing well, getting certificates.'* (local NIE)

The loss of this course, apparently for budgetary reasons, was regarded as a serious blow. Given the popularity of any exercise-related activity, and the opportunities to use this and similar courses for embedding basic and key skills accreditation, this seemed a great shame.

Workshops

The scarcity of NVQ accreditation in the skills-based workshops was regretted by group members. In one NIE group, a prisoner who worked in the tailoring shop felt this was a wasted opportunity. He would have liked something to take away, to demonstrate his new skills:

> *'We're learning to sew, and cutting. But there's no NVQs, no certificates. It's a waste of time. It feels like slave labour. There's nothing to show for it.'* (local)

Offending behaviour programmes

As mentioned earlier, we heard frequently about offending behaviour programmes, when we were asking what else people were doing educationally. They were often referred to in favourable terms.

> 'You address things you know are missing, that need addressing. I'm doing a lot of work on alcohol (abuse). In education you can help yourself.' (local)

However not all were so positive:

> 'Them courses they try to get you to do, they're not going to change my mind about doing crime. I just woke up one day [and decided to stop]. No course makes you think you will give up crime.' (C cat training)

As for so many, the things that really mattered were all going on outside the prison walls.

Just as with the workshops, the division in prison life between formal education (basic skills, academic and creative programmes), offending behaviour programmes and skills-based vocational training seemed pretty arbitrary – and, to many respondents, invisible.

Charity and other learning opportunities

Some mentioned courses available 'through the chapel'. One prisoner-learner at a C Cat training prison had done a course in sign language in this way. A number of charities working in prison were mentioned. We heard about 'Listeners' training (through the Samaritans), and the training in Braille, large-print book-making and wheelchair repair and renovation (through the Inside Out Trust).

Another prisoner mentioned a new Alternatives to Violence Project workshop that had been 'piloted at the weekend'. He was impressed.

> 'It's learning about people and yourself at the same time.' (local)

At another prison there was a rock band in the gym 'to raise money for charity'.

In three of the groups respondents were allowed out on day release to a local college. This gave them a great deal of satisfaction.

Informal learning

A number of other learning opportunities were available, on an ad hoc basis, in some of the prisons.

> 'A lady comes in to do cross-stitch. She's got a shop and sells stuff at reasonable prices – nothing to do with education though.' (women's prison)

> 'One of the chefs does cards and stuff, like for mothers day.' (women's prison)

Other self-help opportunities arose on the wings, too:

> 'Two or three of us took it upon ourselves to teach art and drawing on the wing.' (dispersal)

> 'People just help each other informally in their block. One of my mates helped me write my letters.' (Cat C Training NIE)

2.7 What else prisoners would like to learn and why

Practical and trade courses

Prisoners in all groups gave trade and manual courses top priority:

> *'Not things like sociology and psychology.'*

> *'He doesn't want to touch a classroom environment but give him something he can get his hands to and he'd be alright.'*

> *'A lot of people want manual classes. They don't just want to sit round a desk.'*

> *'Trades, practical courses. Things people could actually make money doing. It's OK doing history but are you going to be able to get a job with it?'*

The over-arching message was clear: prisoners wanted courses to give them skills that had an immediate market value. The assumption that you were more likely, with your record, to get a job working for yourself, was evident.

In discussing practical and trade skills, the most frequently mentioned topics were: cooking and catering, plumbing, electrics, and woodwork. Less often, the groups mentioned hairdressing, manicures, and technical drawing.

Prisoners were particularly interested in gaining qualifications, whether through their work in the prison kitchens, or through specialist training courses.

> *'You could link in food handling for men working in the kitchen with a possible future career. You could get NVQ Catering.'* (C Cat Training)

> *'They could offer something in hospitality – they could train young people to go into catering or having a B and B: something vocational.'* (women's closed)

Plumbing was the second most popular choice. Prisoners thought this was the least available course amongst the construction trade courses on offer across the prison estate. Of all the building trades, it was the one most prisoners thought would provide a good chance of self-employment.

Alongside trade skills, the groups listed a number of creative subjects, with music and sound engineering scoring highest. A number of prisoners cited one particular prison as having excellent facilities:

> *'HMP X have a brilliant room, a recording studio.'* (YOI)

The women's groups wanted crafts:

> *'Needlework, knitting, sewing – all the things you'd expect in a women's prison which women would do at home.'* (women's prison)

Subjects mentioned less often included design, photography and creative writing. Academic courses were cited less often than creative subjects or trade skills, although long-term prisoners were somewhat more interested in these than other groups. The academic subjects most frequently cited were language and psychology, with other courses, such as law, history, geography, and science receiving a few mentions.

We were told that prisoner-learners wanted more access to OU degree level and other higher level courses 'but you've got to figure out how to get it. They're very selective' (dispersal).

The prisoner-learner groups also expressed interest in general courses, including religious studies (e.g., on the Koran), health and personal development (e.g., medical physiology, personal presentation, and the driving test), and vocational topics such as counselling or dental technology.

The loss of evening classes was keenly felt. In some of the prisons, it sounded as though there was a programme on one evening a week, but the full programmes of the past were gone, and were missed. Insofar as group members expressed a view, however, it was that they wanted the opportunity to continue studying in the evenings.

When asked for the one thing he wanted to change about prison education, one prisoner asked for:

> 'Evening classes. If you do something good just before you go to bed, it's fresh in your memory.' (local)

3.   Past Learning Experiences

3.1   Experiences of school

What were thesee prisoners' reflections on their experiences of school?

Some of the replies confounded the easy stereotype of the prisoner as the product of a disrupted education. For instance, in the group in the closed women's prison, three responded positively, two negatively when we asked how they felt about their school days.

There were many, especially in the men's prisons who had had poor experiences:

> *'I truanted from all the schools in London. So they sent me to a special school. One hour of education every day.'* (dispersal)

> *'I was kicked out of three schools. I was kicked out in my first year in A. Thrown out in B. And then thrown out of a school for kids who (were excluded). I accomplished absolutely nothing except wasting 14 years of my life.'* (C cat training)

> *'I used to bunk off. I didn't stay on for the summer for my GCSEs. I didn't think the teaching quality was good. I just got put off what I couldn't do and lost interest. I was in an adolescent hostel: none of them used to go to school, so I used to think: "Why should I?"'* (women's prison)

A number mentioned the harsh environment of residential schools:

> *'You couldn't get through a lesson without somebody getting twisted up [held on the floor in a restraint]. How are you supposed to learn?'* (YOI)

For others again, problems at home (in so far as they were willing to disclose these in the groups) were the most significant feature of their childhood years. Some had overcome considerable obstacles to gain qualifications:

> *'[School was] alright. I used to skive a lot, rebel a bit, but I got most of my exams. I had quite a lot of problems at home. The old man was away a bit so we just went our own way. I followed my older brother. The Social Services chap made me go to school when we set fire to the garden. I got five GCSEs though.'* (Adult and YOI C Cat)

Along with negative memories, there was a significant minority, who felt that school had been beneficial:

> *'I enjoyed school, apart from maths.'* (closed women's)

> *'I loved it till I was 14, then I was pushed too hard. I took exams, ten O levels. I got the three I wanted.'* (C Cat training)

Some also expressed reasons for liking school that were unexpected:

> *'School drew me like a magnet because I got fed. There was a three course lunch. I can still remember my first day. I used sand and stylus etch-a-sketch. Sport was good but it was hard. I did a year of secondary school and then I buggered off to earn money.'* (C Cat training)

There were many who felt the same. School was a bit of an irrelevance. And it was dangerous to be regarded as a swot.

> *'School: messing about is what it's there for. You get branded as a geek and a bookworm.'*

But, 'as an adult you think and see things differently.' (local NIE)

3.2 Experiences of further and higher education

We also asked whether anyone had been to college, and if so, what they had thought of it. In all but two of our groups, there was at least one person who had done some formal post-school learning.

> *'I went to college and did C and G [City and Guilds] in plastering, so I can't complain. I didn't have any chances because I did.'* (adult and YOI C Cat)

Others started YTS courses, though they felt with hindsight that they hadn't always made the most of them:

> *'I went to YTS one day a week to college. It was very good. I did practical stuff. Wages were a tenth of doing manual labour. Now I look back and wish I'd got City and Guilds.'* (local NIE)

To which a fellow group member responded:

> *'If only, if only. In prison you've got an ideal opportunity to try to rectify that.'* (local NIE)

Seven individuals in the prisoner-learner groups told us they were educated to degree level or above:

> *'Back home [overseas]..., I was a part-time lecturer. I've got two Masters degrees, three certificates, three diplomas'.* (local)

> *'Our family came over from [overseas]..... I've had too much education. I loved it, especially university. I studied medicine and neuro-pharmacology at X medical school.'* (local)

There was a very positive attitude towards tertiary education across many of the groups:

> *'College is great... you're treated like an adult. College was the right thing. It's university I want to do.'* (YOI)

In four of the groups there was a recognition that it was expensive to pay for education outside. This led some to reflect that it was worth making the most of every opportunity prison had to offer.

4.   Experience of Education in prison

4.1   Positive and negative aspects of prison education

Positives

Overwhelmingly group members, those in the NIE groups as well as those attending classes, had a high regard for education in prison.

Positives, in prisoner-learners' eyes, included the fact that they were generally there of their own volition:

> 'I've found it much better now because I want to do it.' (women's prison)

> 'In school it was compulsory. Here you can choose.' (dispersal)

The positive differences between this and their own primary and secondary school education were recognised and appreciated:

> 'Here you can work at your own pace.' (women's prison)

> 'At school you work as a class and you feel stupid if you can't keep up.' (women's prison)

> 'It's better in terms of teacher-student ratios.' (dispersal)

> 'In school I couldn't get a proper education. Here they want to help you more. They want to educate you more.' (local)

The one-to-one help made a real difference to the lives of many prisoner-learners:

> 'When I came into gaol I couldn't read and write very good. My letters were, like, two lines: 'Hey Mum. How're you doing?' But then I had one-to-one teaching – a very nice lady – and my letters are good now.' (YOI)

The opportunities to make real changes in your life presented by prison education were also recognised and appreciated:

> 'If you want to do it, it can turn your life around. My friend the Prof next door is doing top stuff. A levels, you get me. He's the only one, mind...' (YOI)

Prison education had many of the advantages of college – and in some respects was even better:

> 'When I was at business studies in [HMP X] it was like being at college. It was terrific, and you looked forward to it. (Dispersal NIE)

> 'It's better here than college. The classes are smaller. There are two teachers. You're not thinking that you want to go off to the butty-shop.' (local)

In addition, the fact that prison education was not charged to the prisoner was appreciated by some.

Negatives

Negative experiences were expressed in terms of styles of teaching, the recruitment of education staff, prison discipline.

In four of the ten education groups, some prisoner-learners felt they were not being treated as adults, both by certain tutors, and by the teaching materials they used:

> *'When you get here they treat you straight away as if you're dumb. There's no other problems: that's it. They treat you like you're children.'* (adult and YOI C Cat)

> *'You're spoken down to: very patronising.'* (women's closed)

> *'The teachers in here need to learn that we're not kids. They need to learn how to teach adults.'* (dispersal)

> *'My lessons remind me of playschool. At other prisons it's different. I was shocked here. Roger Red-nose and all that!'* (adult and YOI C Cat)

Underlying many of these complaints was a sense that they were lowest on the list for quality teaching staff. In one third of the groups we heard that some staff were perceived as below the standard they would expect, say, in school or college. Whilst most seemed to put this down to bad luck, poor selection, or the generally second-rate quality of everything about the prison experience, one young prisoner reflected on some of the difficulties faced by the department in getting staff:

> *'There's a high staff turnover here and a lot of them have no experience of prison. They come from school. They're used to people obeying them.'* (YOI)

A few also identified particular staff who they felt had abused their authority. In two prisons we heard of staff getting involved in the disciplinary system of the prison:

> *'Some teachers like to get you going. If you disagree it's a written warning.'* (Adult and YOI B Cat)

The prisoner-learner groups also spoke of problems caused by the attitudes of other prisoner-learners. In three of the twelve prisoner-learner groups, the attitudes of other prisoners were mentioned as a significant barrier to effective teaching and learning. One group member said there was a lack of commitment:

> *'90% of the lads in the class are just there to avoid doing something else.'* (Cat C training)

Another said it was harder to keep order in prison classes than in school:

> *'Two naughty ones in class. At school, Mum sees the letter. I was scared of the teacher and scared of my parents. But here it bothers us less if we're in trouble. What can they do? Take my TV away?'* (YOI)

Other complaints were about limitations imposed by security or by a lack of resources. Some prisoner-learners felt that they had been subject to unnecessarily restrictions:

> *'It's security they're bothered about which is why I can't do any assessments in case I nick the pliers.'* (adult and YOI C Cat)

Complaints about resources were commonplace. Many compared prisons they had been in, usually to the discredit of the current establishment. Prisoners frequently stated that resources for education were not evenly distributed across the prison estate:

> *'Finances are different in different courses. In my last gaol the art finances were good. They could buy whatever they needed. Here they're not. They don't buy quality paper.'* (dispersal, NIE)

The standard of accommodation varied considerably in the prisons we visited, but prisoner-learners seemed relatively unbothered about dilapidated classrooms and lack of space. It was the quality of what went on in those spaces that mattered most to them. However there were limits. In one prison, there was no toilet for prisoners in the education block and this rankled; in another, apparently, the toilets were closed.

4.2   Relationships with education staff

For many, the staff in prison education departments were outstanding. Prisoner-learners recognised the importance of a good tutor in opening up the joy of learning:

> *'The courses I've enjoyed most, it's the tutor that's been the motivating factor.'* (local)

A number of prisoners, across the system, offered personal tributes to individual tutors.

> *'[X] is phenomenal: he teaches English, sociology, general studies – everything. There's a certain academic structure as to how you do things and he takes a lot of time to help you. Nobody has a bad word to say about him.'* (dispersal)

> *'I can think of three. It's as though they're on a mission to get people to realise their potential and build their self-esteem.'* (local)

Some were touched at the lengths some staff were prepared to go for them:

> *'Staff buy things out of their own pockets. The art teacher hasn't got a budget, but she's getting T-shirts and postcards for us [to create art work]. She's paid £14 just to get those two T-shirts.'* (local)

> *'They bring in materials, books, large-size paper.'* (local)

Staff could have a crucial impact on the way a prisoner-learner adjusted to a long sentence:

> *'The first two years of my life sentence I wanted to die. The staff here slowly, slowly brought me out of my shell. They did their best to encourage me.'* (dispersal)

Some reported having been able to form very good relationships with sympathetic individual staff members:

> *'One teacher here is like a counsellor or a personal tutor. He calms you down. I can tell him what's on my mind.'* (local)

> *'Some teachers are sensitive when you're worried about things on the outside.'* (local)

Other group members explicitly did not want tutors to 'get too chummy.' This prisoner-learner wanted an appropriate level of professional distance to be maintained:

> *'I prefer teachers who act like teachers. They don't really know what it's like for us.'* (local)

The prisoners gained wider insights through their contact with the staff:

> '*I have learned things from the tutor apart from the courses: Tolerance. I had to learn tolerance for my children and grandchildren.*' (local)

It was also seen as helpful that tutors looked on prisoner-learners as regular students.

> '*There's a conscious ethos on this block that we're students, not inmates.*' (local)

> '*The attitude of the teachers matters: they don't treat you like a criminal.*' (adult and YOI B Cat)

> '*They treat you like a normal person.*'

> '*You can forget you are in prison.*' (Women's prison)

4.3   A place apart

Many group members told us that they valued being able to put a bit of physical distance between themselves and the rest of the prison, the wings, the staff, the routines.

> '*It takes you off the wing and away from prison staff. You need to get away from them.*'

> '*It's a better atmosphere down here than on the wing.*'

> '*It's nice. It's not rowdy.*' (local)

A number commented on the relative sanctuary afforded by the education department in an otherwise bleak environment.

> '*This is a pretty miserable prison. This is the only place, apart from the chapel, you get a release from the awful surroundings.*' (local)

> '*This is the only place I've felt comfortable in, felt stable.*' (dispersal)

> '*If I hadn't come to the education department I think I would have hung myself. And going to the chapel for a cup of tea and a biscuit. I look forward to the small things.*' (local)

5.   The Value of Education

What did prisoners think was important about education?

The prisoners' responses ranged from a fairly pragmatic skills-based appraisal to a sense that education was essential for getting on in the world:

> 'It's really important, really, because everyone needs maths, English, and computers and that.' (local)

> 'Knowledge is power. The guy who owns the newspapers can tell people what to do. (Adult and YOI, Cat B)

> 'The more education I've got, the bigger my house is going to be.' (local NIE)

> 'I don't want to be a down and out bum.' (adult and YOI B cat NIE)

5.1   Making progress: using the time

In 10 out of the 12 prisoner-learner groups, prisoners said they wanted to make good use of their time in prison. A sense of making progress, even though the rest of life was standing still, was seen as vital to maintaining morale:

> 'Using the time properly: it gives you encouragement.' (local)

> 'If you're in here for a time, you go out the same mental age as you came in, if you're not careful.' (dispersal)

> 'I'm progressing. I'm not wasting time.' (local)

> 'It's good to make a positive out of a negative.' (C Cat training)

One put it this way:

> For me, coming to education helps to pass the time. Time drags if you're doing nothing. I can't break out, I don't want to be crawling out, I want to be walking out.' (local)

Keeping your mind occupied was also seen as important:

> 'It stops you brooding about past mistakes.' (dispersal)

> 'Keeping your brain active' was seen by many as the primary reason for coming to classes. A number of prisoners, from across the groups, voiced a fear that their brains would rot, if they just 'vegetated' in their cells.

> 'If you don't do education you deteriorate.' (C Cat training)

A sense of achievement was seen as invaluable by most:

> 'I couldn't read and write when I came to prison and I've got GCSEs now.' (Women's open)

Some said they were motivated by the feeling that learning was something they could do for themselves, not for the prison, or because it was required, or for other people:

> *'I feel that I need to do this for me, for nobody else, just for me.'* (local)

For others, it appeared that education was an unqualified good in itself.

> *'It's essential: education just is.'* (local)

When asked what he liked most about going to 'education' one responded:

> *'Learning, Miss, learning. I've learned a bit by coming down here.'* (C Cat training)

However, not all were convinced that improving their education whilst in prison would do much for their chances of avoiding reconviction on release:

> *'No matter how much education you do, all that good stuff you've done in gaol, it goes at the gates. 70-80 per cent of prisoners do what they did before, straight away. 10 per cent try not to, but will go back to crime. 10 per cent stay out of crime.'* (C cat training)

5.2   Education as a life-changing force

In almost every group, there was a least one contributor who believed in the power of education to change lives. Moreover, many recognised that a prison sentence represented a valuable opportunity for those who wanted a second chance at learning, and the choices it could bring:

> *'It's the only time you can do it, while you're in prison. When you're leading a life of crime on the streets there's no time for it. But if you have an education, you have the choice.'* (local)

Education was seen by some as the route out of their previous lives. As one young man saw it, it was helpful to see fellow inmates as a reminder of what the future could hold in store, unless he took action:

> *'I look at some people older than me and I don't want to be like them. Education and training? It's the only way I can do it.'* (Adult and YOI Cat B)

Some saw education as a route to employment:

> *'I was unemployed for 15 years before I came in jail. I'm hoping I can get some kind of a career out of it.'* (Cat C training)

> *'I'm geared up to get a job when I get out. I haven't had a job since I left school. I want to do it so I don't end up back here.* (Cat C Training)

The YOI group came closest to acknowledging that education could be a life-changing force – though this was mainly the view of one strong-minded individual.

> *'Prison is a poor man's college. This is the worst gaol, but if you were in HMP X or HMP Y you could turn your life around.'* (YOI)

The speaker was challenged by another member of the group:

> *'You're trying to say prison education can stop crime?'*

He responded by drawing a link between education and a change of identity:

> *'No, but it can reduce it. I was a kid when I started selling drugs and robbing and stuff. I would like to improve my life. But if you are still on this gangster-life image you'll be back here.'* (YOI)

Some individuals were motivated by the prospect of qualifications and jobs, and no-one wanted to return to gaol. However, for most individuals, although giving up crime might be a consequence of their new learning, it was not something they mentioned as the most important thing about education.

5.3   Prisoner-learners' reasons for enrolling in classes

Some prisoner-learners said they did not feel like they had a choice:

> 'There's nothing else to do.'

> 'If you don't work you have to go to education unless you're ill.' (Women's prison)

For others there were more positive motivations. Some linked to particular circumstances and interests:

> 'My ambition is to get a PhD in Philosophy. I'm not going anywhere. I've got 25 years, life.' (dispersal)

Most were more down-to-earth:

> 'I want to improve my prospects for when I get out.' (Cat C Adult and YOI)

One prisoner-learner put it slightly differently:

> 'When they ask me, "What have you done in gaol?" I don't want to end up saying, "Well, I watched a bit of day time TV."' (YOI)

The same opinion kept coming up, across all the prisoner-learner groups: using the time to better yourself and to improve your future employment prospects was the main motivation for study.

Qualifications mattered to some:

> 'Very important – you need qualifications to get a job.' (local)

But not to all: passing the time, in a way that would boost your self-esteem, was seen by a few to be more important.

> 'In Art, if a teacher says, "You'll get a certificate" I lose motivation.' (Adult and YOI Cat B)

Similarly, the new skills and choices education offered were seen to be more valuable than qualifications, per se.

> 'The actual qualifications you get may not get you a job, but [education] does help you to consider alternatives....It's the process education gives you that's important.' (dispersal)

In two groups, we heard how much it mattered to prisoners that their certificates were from outside providers: that they did not mention the prison in which they had been gained. This was important to them.

5.4   Improving employment prospects upon release

There was a marked scepticism, some would say realism, about their chances of employment on release.

> 'It's going to be hard to get a job whatever qualifications you've got. Prison tars your record.' (Cat C training prison)

But qualifications as an indicator of your sticking power, and your general abilities, were valued by most, even if they did not seem to offer a highway to a job.   One prisoner, doing distance learning with a Christian college, remarked:

> '*I don't think they're going to give me a job running a church. But it counts for something if you show you've got the competence and ability to study to that level.*' (local)

6. Prisoners' Perceptions of Others' Attitudes Towards Education

What did the prisoners feel other people thought about their education? We asked prisoner-learners and the NIE groups to respond with their understanding of the views of other prisoners, prison officers, probation officers, governors, and families and friends.

Other prisoners

> 'Every man's different. I can't speak for anyone else.' (local – NIE)

In each discussion group, and particularly when prisoners were serving longer sentences, there was a discernible attitude of tolerance and respect for other prisoners. Whilst group members were often ready to judge prison staff, they were far less likely to pronounce upon, or prescribe for, other prisoners.

A few prisoners, however, doubted the motives of peers who pursued education.

> 'Most people in the education department are skivers. Very few come to learn.' (local)

In one group, where we interviewed adult and young prisoners together, the group was extremely tolerant towards a young prisoner with special needs who was disruptive. However, some of the older men expressed exasperation with younger prisoner-learners:

> 'The younger kids don't bother – all they've got is a small sentence so they don't want to do it (education). They just talk about doing their next job. Kids are kids. Some people don't want to be changed.' (local – NIE)

Some of the older prisoner-learners resented the 'zoo' atmosphere that they thought characterised the education block when the young offenders came in. But a younger man, recently transferred from a YOI to an adult gaol, saw things the other way round:

> 'The old guys – the crim club – just want an easy time.' (Cat C training – NIE)

What did prisoners think were the attitudes of prison staff towards education? We asked the prisoner-learner groups to discuss their perceptions about how other groups, including prison officers, management, and their families and friends, viewed education in prison. Their positive and negative impressions were interestingly similar, in respect of each of the staff groups.

Prison officers

The majority verdict was that prison officers were just not interested in education, or anything rehabilitative, for their charges:

> 'Many think it's a cushy way of spending your sentence.' (women's prison)

> 'There's a touch of sarcasm. The officers think you should have learned to read and write at school.' (C Cat Training prison)

On rare occasions, a prisoner-learner voiced a suspicion that officers were deliberately sabotaging educational opportunities for inmates:

> 'One officer brought down only two or three people. I thought that was terrible. He said no-one was ready. He said the sooner we have 24 hour bang-up the better. There were only three people on classes last week.' (local)

Elsewhere, there was little evidence that prisoner-learners were having difficulty getting to classes.

Some contempt for the officers' educational attainments was apparent too, in several of the groups.

> *'They only need to know the difference between clockwise and anti-clockwise.'* (dispersal)

As was the perception that officers felt threatened by inmates' attainments:

> *'The [officers] don't want to see you doing good. They hate it. You come along with a great A level book and they haven't a GCSE...'* (YOI)

> *'They can't handle an educated prisoner.'* (local)

Another negative impression was that officers were more interested in army-style discipline and controlling prisoners than they were in education and rehabilitation:

> *'It's all written warnings: if you get three of them you get 24 hour bang up. If you're a minute late, a second late, wrong sort of towel, a bowl in my cell...'* (adult and YOI Cat B)

Alongside the negative comments about how officers viewed education, were more positive reflections:

> *'[The officers] stress it's important: the top priority for employers is English and maths and IT. They encourage you to do it.'* (YOI and adult C cat)

> *'One of the officers said, "Good luck" when he heard I had an exam. I thought 'Bloody hell are you serious?' He said he was.'* (local)

And, again, differing attitudes were acknowledged and respected:

> *'It depends on the officers – how they see you. Some don't care whether you do it (education) or not. Others don't want to see you back here – the ones that care.'* (local)

> *'It varies. They're as mixed a bunch as this group here.'* (local)

This more appreciative attitude towards prison officers was expressed in seven of the twelve prisoner-learner groups, by at least one contributor. However, in every group, the majority view seemed to be that prison officers were not interested in education for prisoners at all. One learner in particular saw the negative attitudes of some staff as part of a structural problem:

> *'In an organisation where staff are not well educated they don't value education. You've got to dramatically improve the education of the managers. Then they'd value the education of the officers.'* (dispersal NIE)

Workshop staff

There were at least four types of workshop in operation in the prisons we visited: workshops making goods for the prison estate (e.g., bedsheets, jeans), workshops undertaking commercial contracts, which were making money for the prison (tea-bag packing, light fitting assembly, airline flightbag packing), vocational training workshops (painting and decorating, carpentry) and charity workshops (braille and large print books, wheelchair repair). It was also clear that prisoners were working in other sorts of context in the prisons, for instance in the kitchens, or farms and gardens. Staff there sometimes featured in their comments, too.

Again, the estimation of workshop staff's interest in educating prisoners varied greatly. However the perceptions were largely positive:

> *'The staff are keen to get you out of there. They encourage you to better yourself in prison.'* (local)

> *'I work in a charity workshop. My gaffer over there hasn't got a problem with me doing the IT course. He likes to see me learning.'* (dispersal)

In one workshop, run by the charity the Inside Out Trust, the task was rewarding, and prisoners enjoyed feeling they had made a difference to the lives of people less fortunate than themselves. However, as we found elsewhere, it was the individual staff member and the quality of the relationships they had built up with prisoners which proved the greatest motivator.

The few negative remarks tended to focus on the relative primacy of workshops over education in the prison hierarchy, as prisoners perceived it:

> *'They're a bit jealous: they'd like more people in the workshops.'* (local)

> *'When it comes to this nick, reading and writing is not as important as going to the workshops and getting money.'* (dispersal)

Probation officers

Probation officers attracted almost universally negative comment. It was not that they were seen as hostile to education: rather that they were not seen at all.

Comments were pretty uniform, from all parts of the estate:

> *'Do we have probation officers?'* (women's prison)

> *'The who? Who are they? We never see them.'* (local)

> *'I've been here 16 months. I've never seen one.'* (adult and YOI cat B)

> *'Haven't seen mine for five years.'* (dispersal)

In so far as they were a presence for group members, probation officers seemed to be more interested in them completing offending behaviour programmes than improving basic skills, vocational training, or developing their education.

In only four of the 22 groups (including both prisoner-learners and those not in education) were there some positive remarks about an individual probation officer's interest in education.

Prison governors

In some prisons the governors were seen as interested, in others not.

'Governor [X] kept pottery for us' said one in a local jail, which seemed to have had a good track record in keeping its creative programmes running, to the satisfaction of inmates.

In the YOI, no-one offered a positive view of governors' opinions about education. On the contrary, some of the young offenders felt that governors were only interested in avoiding the sort of adverse publicity that might result from a suicide in their prison:

> *'You mean the suits? We don't know nothing about no governors, the ones in suits. We don't see them.'*

> *'They come in your cell when you arrive and say: 'Don't hang yourself' and then they leave.'* (YOI)

There was a clearer sense in some adult groups of the factors influencing a governing governor's view of education. Key performance targets and their impact made an appearance:

> *'The Prison Service has targets to reach in level one, so they're interested in that.'*

To which a fellow group member responded:

> *'That's why you get kicked off when you get qualifications.'* (Adult and YOI C Cat)

In another prison, one group member thought that education was 'a low budget way of getting their targets' for governors. Talking of the decision to close a popular sports course in a local prison, a prisoner described one of the operational headaches for governors, as:

> *'Governors think it's a good idea but they need people to work in the workshops because of outside contracts. Education is losing them money.'* (local)

One of the women's groups expressed admiration for one of the governors:

> *'If you need to do your education, [governor x] is very supportive,'* said one.

Similarly, a prisoner-learner in a different establishment spoke of the encouragement he had received from a governor:

> *'I've been in and out for ages. I was always down the block. Now I'm on education. He eggs me on and says, "Go on and do it".'* (adult and YOI cat B)

The encouragement of particular individuals appears to have made a real difference to raising the educational aspirations of some inmates. Throughout the study, prisoner-learners spoke of the importance of positive role models for them. Whether it was an encouraging governor, a tutor, an officer, a family member or friend, or another prisoner or ex-prisoner, the significance of particular people in inspiring, supporting and encouraging learning efforts was manifest. The value of a person who is willing to show that they believe in the prisoner-learner and who can see a potential that the prisoner themselves may not see, cannot be under-estimated.

Family and friends

The influence of families, friends, partners and significant others in shaping prisoners' perceptions of the value of education, and in encouraging their efforts, was undeniable. In a few cases however, this appeared negative:

> *'They don't think a shit about it.'* (adult and YOI Cat B)

> *'My family were happy about me doing painting and decorating 'cos I can get a job. They don't care about this education.'* (C Cat Training)

But the majority ranged from the neutral to the positive:

> *'My partner's quite impressed. It's a chance to better yourself. If you don't come to prison there's some things you wouldn't do.'* (women's prison)

> *'They're always pleased if I get on.'* (adult and YOI C cat)

Some, however, showed their anguish at their families' situations:

> *'My Mum wants to see me succeeding and going to college. It did break her heart to have me in here.'* (adult and YOI Cat B)

For some prisoners it made a valuable and meaningful link with their own children possible:

> *'I can ask my boy about his GCSEs – but he's in that monosyllabic phase just now.'* (dispersal)

> *'I send a lot of artwork home and I write stories for the children. My Missus is a primary school teacher and she encourages me to.'* (C CatTraining)

Others mentioned valuable knock-on effects for the wider family, alongside the discovery of a source of pride and satisfaction for themselves. As one long-term prisoner put it:

> *'I never really went to school. I spent most of my time on the street committing crime. Here I've found something within myself (art and painting) and my family's proud of me. It's reflected on my little brother. He's gone to college to do art and design. So it's reflected on my family as well.'* (Dispersal)

In the women's groups, there was a markedly positive response to this question:

> *'I think they're quite proud.'*

> *'My daughter, she's 18 and she's encouraged me to do a BA.'*

> *'My Dad's really supportive.'* (women's prison)

The overwhelming message was of the importance of support and encouragement from outside, and of the reciprocal pride that some prisoners took in their achievements, as reflected in they eyes of their families. As one long-term prisoner-learner put it:

> *'It's important for me to earn their respect back.'* (dispersal)

It seemed as though some prisons were actively encouraging a two-way exchange of work – for instance where parenting courses were offered, and the prisoners were encouraged to write stories for their children. We did not hear of any more explicit opportunities for family and friends to congratulate prisoners on their achievements, such as awards ceremonies, but that is not to say they did not exist. We were struck by how deeply prisoners appreciated the external support, particularly for those who were achieving external accreditation for the first time in their lives. This seemed to offer a real opportunity for future innovation and development.

7.   Release and Resettlement

As group members saw it, education and training were not regarded by prison managers as the best use of their time in prison. Given the Prison Service's recent focus on resettlement, we were interested to know how prisoners themselves felt about impending release.

7.1   The benefit of education

We asked group members whether they thought that having attended classes in prison would help them on release. Again, there was a mixed response. Broadly, they thought it would. But there was a division between how it would help themselves and the family and how it would affect employment prospects. As regards the former, there was a broad consensus that their educational achievements in prison would help:

> 'Yes. I'm not fooling myself, but it helps your self-esteem. It's going to help you, isn't it?' (dispersal)

> 'It helps me a lot. It will help with my home life. I've got five kids. The eldest is nine, the youngest is five months.' (local)

> 'Good for your kids when you get home. You feel proud. Better as a person.' (local)

For these men, being able to read to their children, and take an interest in their schoolwork, as well as feeling 'better as a person', was going to be important in re-establishing themselves within their families on release. One group member, thinking about the potential relationship difficulties to which all prisoners are subject, added:

> 'They have stuff on crime and offending behaviour, crime and sex. There should be something on crime and relationships. Because basically if you commit a crime you aren't going to have any relationships are you?' (adult and YOI C Cat)

For others, there were good pragmatic reasons why the basic skills learned in prison were going to help in resettlement.

> 'It will help me. I've got my own business. I used not to be able to work it all out. Now I can do a bit in my head. I've got to carry on.' (local)

A number hoped that their educational achievements would influence parole boards in their favour. But, depressingly, it seemed as though parole boards did not always get to hear of a prisoner's academic successes:

> 'I've been on six parole boards and they've not known anything about what I've done.' (dispersal)

There were some dissenting voices, however. One man, whose levels of functional literacy and numeracy may well have been reasonably good before he came to prison, expressed some cynicism about what he saw as naivety amongst some fellow prisoners:

> 'They're all saying because they've done a bit of education their head's been turned. This hasn't changed me a bit. Education isn't going to change things.' (adult and YOI C Cat)

And one woman had been more struck by the corrupting influence of the informal education provided by a prison sentence than by anything provided by the regime itself:

> *'It's not going to help me. I can't think of anything in prison that will help me on the outside. I've got a lot of education in the wrong way. I didn't know things about credit cards. If I wanted a life of crime I could have it. This is college for it!'* (women's closed)

We heard views along the lines of Henry Fielding's remark about 'seminaries of vice' expressed in four other groups.

7.2   Continuing with education after release

In every group of prisoner-learners, at least one person wanted to continue with some kind of education or training after release. However there were differing perceptions about its likelihood and worth: in some a flame had been kindled, in others, it was seen as a luxury or an irrelevance.

> *'Education's about interest. People might want to carry on with what they've started here when they get outside, if it's sparked an interest they never knew they had.'* (dispersal)

> *'Yes I'm going to carry on with maths and English, even if it's just once a week.'* (local)

> *'My OU tutor invited me to apply for a research place in Milton Keynes when I get out. It was really nice.'* (dispersal)

In two groups, prisoners mentioned other ex-prisoners they knew who had gone on and made the grade, educationally. These had clearly provided inspirational role models. One spoke admiringly of:

> *'A 12-year sentence drug dealer who started in '97. Now he's a PhD working in university.'* (Local)

At least three, from different groups, were getting ready to resume university studies that had been disrupted by prison. Two prisoners told us that they were focused upon new careers, but had been unable to pursue the qualifications they needed in prison. Both were clear that they would need further training in their chosen work.

> *'No prisons do it. I've got to wait till I get discharged. I intend doing it for a living. If I'm going to work and stop thieving then that is what I've got to do.'* (dispersal NIE)

Another, however, reacted negatively to the idea of any further study:

> *'I'm going to get a job and that's it. Don't want to do no college.'* (women's prison)

For many, earning enough money to get by was the main pre-occupation:

> *'No, I've got to make money. I've got five kids.'* (dispersal)

> *'Most of us have kids and need to earn. Me going to college and them going to college will be tough.'* (women's prison)

> *'It's quite expensive. £600 for A levels.'* (YOI)

But more than half of the groups said they recognised the difficulties of life after release and the demands of other more pressing problems. A prisoner-learner whose contributions suggested he knew some of these problems at first hand commented:

> *'You have so many plans before you get out, but when you do get out you think – what is all this? There's so much to do to get by.'* (adult and YOI C Cat)

Another reflected on the dislocation of release, and the upheaval to get your life back together, saying:

> *'It's hard to come out of prison and do further study. If you haven't got a settled life, it's really hard'.* (C Cat training)

A young prisoner was realistic about the temptations awaiting him on return to his community:

> *'No. I wouldn't be able to stick with it. I'll end up mixing with the wrong crowd again. I want a job, not education and training.'* (Adult and YOI B Cat NIE)

In a third of the prisoner-learner groups, members said that they wanted to get their education sorted out whilst they were inside.

> *'I was hoping to get it all here, so I don't have to.'* (YOI)

> *'If you're doing 15 years you should complete your education now.'* (dispersal)

It sounded as though, for most in our study, the prospect of getting help with any educational goals they might have on release seemed remote, when, in their opinion, the prison lost interest in you as soon as you went out of the gate. Even getting a clear release date seemed a problem, for some:

> *'Nothing is very organised for when you come out. They can't even get the dates right.'* (local)

7.3   Getting jobs

There were differing perceptions on whether education which they had undertaken in prison would help with employment. These ranged from a determination that it had a key role, through to a desire for more vocational training and employer-led schemes in prison, to a cynicism about chances and a corresponding resignation about the inevitability of self-employment – unless you were lucky enough to have a sympathetic previous employer or a job with your family.

A minority of prisoners were reasonably optimistic that their educational achievements in prison would help them in their search for a job:

> *'I think it will help if you want to get a job like health or social care or sports.'* (C Cat training)

> *'When you get released there's a good chance there'll be a job waiting for you [if you've done classes]. It looks like you've tried to get yourself educated.'* (local NIE)

One commented on the useful self-discipline that coming to classes had taught him:

> *'I'm used to getting up in the morning now, so I can get up and go to work.'* (adult and YOI C Cat)

But gloom was quick to emerge in most of the groups. There was a lot of fatalism about the likely success of your application if you were competing in an open market:

> *'I don't think it makes a blind bit of difference when you get out. You're still a criminal. I went for a few jobs and I was honest' [and didn't get them].* (local NIE)

> *'Who wants to employ an ex-prisoner? You have to either start up your own business or lie.'* (C cat training)

> *'It's a pity that once you've been to prison you're unlikely to get a job. I spent nine and a half years in university.'* (local)

There was also the sense that, as an ex-offender, you would only be offered undesirable jobs anyway:

> *'My co-defendant can't find a job because he's got that tag that he's an ex-offender. He... did qualifications, and he's been out for seven months and he's working behind a bar.'* (C Cat training NIE)

> *'I'll have a degree behind me when I leave, but I'll have to apply for a factory job. I've got a 22-year gap in employment. I'm not doing education with a job in mind.'* (C cat training)

Although the acquisition of functional literacy and numeracy skills was by and large seen as necessary to get any job in today's market, and IT skills were deemed indispensable for any kind of office job, the prisoners who spoke to us did not, for the most part, think these things were enough. There was still the problem of their criminal conviction. For many, therefore, the opportunity either to work cash-in-hand, in the construction industry, or else to work for themselves, seemed the most sensible options. Once again, what they wanted were more trade and manual skills courses, and places on those courses, in prison.

Encouraging Learning in Prison

1.   Prisoners' recommendations for change

• 'One thing that could be changed.'

We asked all group members: if they could change one thing about education for prisoners, what would it be?

More resources was the top priority. As one group member put it:

> *'Resources. Drug rehab is expensive but cost-effective. Preventing accidents costs money BUT less than the accidents would. It's more expensive in the long run not to provide education for prisoners.'* (local)

In addition to this plea, more and different activities, greater personal choice, and better timetabling, were sought. Evening classes were mentioned in five groups. More part time places were also in demand, so that you could work and study at the same time, and so was an end to waiting lists.

More accreditation, and vocational skills training leading to qualifications were mentioned repeatedly. More courses and places were regularly requested. Schemes sponsored by employers, leading to jobs on release, were particularly welcomed:

> *'If you're qualified, you can go out. You're not always looking over your shoulder expecting a knock on the door.* (local NIE)

> *'I'd offer more vocational skills. Something you can use and earn money.'* (women's prison)

> *'More links to the job market.'* (Cat C training)

Improved facilities were mentioned by a few:

> *'A larger building for the education department. It used to be twice the size. This is just a prefab building. They can extend it...'* (women's prison)

IT and computing. Where facilities were not good, access to good computer training was desired, so that prison education was not left in some time warp of its own.

'Kitchen' and 'cooking' were frequently mentioned and desired.

More and better teaching staff were regularly mentioned, as was training for non-teaching staff:

> *'Until the officers value education for themselves they'll find it difficult to value it for others. Until that's sorted, there won't be any change.'* (dispersal)

Better teacher-student relations: One specifically mentioned:

> *'... more interaction between teachers and prisoners. Like more, "How can we help each other?" Like I did a cost-benefit on prisons, and the teacher said that was good coming from my perspective.'* (adult and YOI C cat)

A tough approach to time-wasters: In three groups, a more draconian approach to those who did not want to learn was recommended:

> *'There are a lot of classes in which not a lot of work gets done. This is wasting teachers' time. They are dedicated. They need back-up when they want to remove people.'* (dispersal)

One prisoner was clear about what to do:

> *'I'd put the wages up and give people a test every now and then. If they're not paying attention, throw them out.'* (local)

There was a conflict of opinions between this type of view, and that expressed in another group of younger prisoners, where there was a strong wish to make education 'compulsory.'

Encouraging and supporting education on the wings: this, and the wish to extend help to those who really needed it but were not coming forward, was mentioned several times.

Better pay and improved access to gym were frequent requests.

The exemption of education from the mechanics of the IEP scheme was a particular wish amongst the longer-term prisoners

Time and space for breaks: tea breaks were seen as highly desirable. In some prisons, there were breaks and others not. As mentioned above, the toilets were shut in one prison's education department, and had been taken out in another. In a third, there was a request for a phone (because you can never use one otherwise) and a shower (because you can only use one at weekends otherwise, and then the water's cold.)

Better communications with prisoners: A suggestions box was proposed, and regular meetings with prisoners to canvass their views.

Better information. The education department needed to let prisoners know what was available. A newsletter was regarded as a good idea. In several groups, there seemed to be a lack of any idea about what was possible, except by word of mouth.

2.   *Encouragers and discouragers: process issues*

When prisoners were asked what they wanted, they came up with a clear list. Most wanted more of what was there already, with a better focus on the inmate rather than the prison. However many in the groups had not recently enjoyed any other experiences of formal education elsewhere, so had nothing for comparison.

Our study revealed a little more about what seemed to encourage, and what seemed to discourage learning in prison. As we interviewed more groups, we became aware of emerging divisions between process-type issues and people issues when considering what encouraged, and what discouraged such learning.

The process issues covered both prison-wide, and education department-focused matters. Unfortunately all prison-wide issues seemed to function as 'discouragers'.

Induction and assessment

We heard an inconsistent story, across the estate, about initial assessments. It was not clear that all prisoners' learning needs were assessed as a matter of course. In some prisons, we heard that needs were carefully assessed, and appropriate classes offered. In other places, it did not sound as though the assessment was so thorough, or that the identified need led to an appropriate place being offered. And in some prisons, neither seemed to have happened. Where these assessments were done, there was still no automatic follow-through to meeting identified educational needs, even in the case of prisoners with perceived literacy and numeracy difficulties.

Applications

Particularly in the local prisons, the applications procedure seemed both perplexing, and often fallible. Far too many applications did not seem to have got through, or at least did not result in any education. Where in the chain they were getting stuck was unclear, but from the prisoners' point of view, the process started on the wings.

Getting to the education department at all was perceived to be the major stumbling block for many, especially in the local prisons, or in the dispersal prisons where security issues created problems. It was not in general suggested that the education departments were deliberately thwarting prisoners' aspirations, however; rather that the links between the prison's administrative systems were not good.

Pay

As mentioned above, and as has been canvassed in other studies, prisoners felt particularly strongly about poor rates of pay, relative to other work-party choices available in that establishment. This certainly discouraged many from study, regardless of any assessments that may have indicated serious educational needs.

Prison timetables

Timetables can drive activities rather than the other way round. We were dismayed by some of the trade-offs we learned that prisoners had to make to get to classes: having to choose between coming to classes and getting to the library or the gym – and in one case even getting a shower and a kit change. We heard of prisoners having to choose between education and phoning their families, or education and exercise. We also heard of inflexible unlocking schedules, with too little time allowed for breakfast and washing in the morning, which sometimes meant that people were not escorted to classes if they were a moment late in getting ready.

Cell study

Some of the difficulties of studying in the cells were new to us: the omni-presence of in-cell TV, for example, and the difficulty of studying with an unsympathetic cell-mate. We heard of apparently arbitrary rulings on self-study equipment and materials in cells, which seemed to differ within the same prison, let alone between different prisons of the same security category. All these were significant discouragers.

Sentence planning

The low priority for education in sentence-planning terms, as seen through prisoners' eyes, was depressing, as was the lack of any consistent planning for educational progression, both through the sentence and after release. We were struck that target-setting was not presented as a joint or at least negotiated activity. Prisoners were 'given' targets.

Offending behaviour programmes

We were particularly struck by the apparently impermeable regime-driven boundaries between education and OBPs, especially where the latter were sentence plan targets, and the former was not.

Vocational training

Sometimes education and vocational training seemed mutually exclusive. The separation between the education department and the workshops, on the one hand, and the gym, on the other, seemed total. We heard of trade training workshops being closed to accommodate contract workshops, carrying out the same tasks but without accreditation (because numbers had had to be restricted where accreditation was a feature). Alternatively, we heard of work which could have been accredited, for instance in the kitchens or gardens, not being so. We heard of few examples of activities where basic skills accreditation was being woven in to vocational training or activities, but this could have been because prisoners did not think to mention it, and it was not a question we asked explicitly.

Education departmental issues

The picture here was not so depressing, and practice varied more widely across the prisons we visited. In general, prisoners were far readier to give education staff the benefit of the doubt, if, for instance, it was not clear where in the system a problem was occurring. Nevertheless, there were still certain process factors concerning education departments which seemed to function mainly as discouragements to learning.

Availability of places

Particularly in the local prisons, there seemed real difficulties about providing enough places, in most subjects, for those who wanted them. Long waiting lists, where they existed, were discouraging.

The curriculum offered

The variability of the curriculum between prisons was striking. Different courses were offered, leading to different qualifications. This seemed particularly unfortunate, since regular transfer is a feature of prison life for any but the shortest sentenced prisoners. It led to real difficulties in progression, a stop-start feel to prisoners' learning, with courses abandoned half way, work left behind, and a need to start again from scratch – if indeed this was possible in the new prison.

Similarly striking was the extent to which some prisons seemed to be offering little but target-driven basic skills courses, whilst others appeared able to be far more responsive to what prisoners wanted to study. Similarly, some prisons seemed to be finding creative ways to weave basic skills accreditation into more appealing subject areas.

Lack of sufficient provision for Open University and other distance learning opportunities was mentioned, but where these chances were available, they were great encouragers.

Transfer of records

We heard frequently that prisoners' educational records did not follow them on transfer. This often meant they had to start again, at the new prison, sometimes re-taking qualifications they had already obtained. This was a significant discourager.

Alternative means of delivery

Where assistance with meeting educational needs other than through traditional class-room teaching was available, this acted as a significant encourager. Prisoners were particularly supportive of peer learning schemes, where these existed, and of help to study on their own, in their cells, in workshops, and wherever else they found themselves during the prison day. They also welcomed flexible timetabling, allowing them to work part-time and study part-time too.

Where opportunities to combine educational achievement with other aspects of their life in the prison existed, these counted as significant encouragers, as this example shows:

> *'I'm race relations rep on our wing. I did a presentation that served two purposes. It was about the race relations, and it counted as half a module for computer accreditation.'* (local)

Equipment and materials

Where decent IT, art, and other equipment was available, this was much appreciated. Lack of internet access was regretted. We heard little about other teaching materials, other than a general regret about shortages, the occasional disparaging reference to childish literacy material and exercises, and to a lack of black history and multi-cultural reference materials.

Library facilities

Where access to the library was facilitated through the education department, and the service was good, this was a significant encourager.

The ethos

In the majority of prisoner-learner groups, the work culture in the education department was a major encourager. Being treated as a 'normal human being', a 'student, not a criminal', was highly valued, as was the studious atmosphere. There was the sense that, for some, this was a place of refuge in an otherwise bleak and dehumanising environment. In the few prisons where prisoner-learners felt they were back at school, or where prison rules and discipline seemed as present as ever, this was discouraging, but not totally so. There were still more applicants than places.

3. Encouragers and discouragers: People issues

The respondents spoke about the importance of the attitudes of a key group of people. These would determine the extent to which prisoners were encouraged to learn, or discouraged from trying.

Education staff: we heard frequently about the inspirational effect of good tutors, who were passionate about their subjects, who believed in individuals and in their ability to progress. These were amongst the most significant encouragers we came across. However, prisoners sometimes felt there were not enough staff of this quality teaching in the prison. Being treated 'like children' was a definite discourager.

Other staff in the prison: these often served as discouragers, although there were honourable exceptions.

Prison officers' attitudes to education

The groups spoke about the importance of the messages that staff gave about the value of education, particularly the officers. The negative impression prisoners had of the views of prison staff about education was disheartening. As well as disparaging and patronising attitudes towards prisoners with basic literacy needs, we heard of some hostility to educational attainment, particularly if the prisoner was then seen as an intellectual threat. However, other examples were cited of officers whose support was deeply appreciated by particular prisoners.

Family and friends outside

We heard about the value of support from outside, both from inspiring role models, and from people who cared about you, and mattered to you. These functioned as significant encouragers.

Other prisoners

Other prisoners could function either as discouragers (the unsympathetic cell-mate, or the disruptive class member) or as encouragers (the inspiring role model, showing what was possible). The attitudes of peers were certainly significant, either way.

The learners' own attitudes

Past experiences of education coloured how you regarded things. If you wanted to make up for lost time, this could encourage you to learn in prison. But if you had had a low regard for your initial experience of education, this could form a barrier to learning – especially if elements of the experience offered in prison reminded you strongly of school. However, the growth of self-esteem made possible by educational achievement functioned as the best encourager of them all.

> *'It feels good when you do something you couldn't do before.'* (local)

People and attitudes seemed more important, to most of the groups, in determining how they saw education in prison than some of the traditional 'barriers to learning' about which we asked. Classroom materials and furnishing, and group sizes, for example, attracted less interest and passion in the responses than was evidenced in contributions on the topics above. As long as these were 'good enough', it seemed, they were of relatively minor importance: this was so whether the rooms were obviously brand new and freshly painted, or cramped, battered and peeling. It was the attitudes that counted.

4. Overview

As the study progressed, we became increasingly aware of some of the difficulties facing all concerned, prisoners, staff and outside providers, in promoting satisfying learning opportunities for prisoners. Some of the difficulties that prisoners described were new to us, and some were depressingly familiar. At the root of it all, however, was the sense that there was no rationale to the provision. Education and training felt like an add-on, an after-thought, unlike, by contrast, the better-resourced and higher profile offending behaviour programmes which seemed central to the regime. Despite the highly appreciated efforts of some of the education staff, and some of the inspiring and exciting work that prisoners talked about, there was a desultory, second-best feel to their accounts of the status of education in prison life as a whole. As things stood, education seemed just too far down the list, in the scale of the things that mattered.

> *'It should be looked upon – if you're trying to better yourself, it's better doing education than putting dirty washing in a washing machine.'* (dispersal NIE)

It is possible that the Prison Service may traditionally have understated some of the difficulties it faces in delivering education to prisoners. In what other setting would a provider be attempting to meet the needs of quite such a diverse range of learners? From non-readers with special educational needs to post-graduates, from juveniles to septuagenarians, the Prison Service has to work with them all.

However, in order to make the significant investment needed to manage such a range, decisions have to be made about what prison education is for. If it is seen primarily as a remedial activity, to tackle perceived skills deficits at the basic level, then it would be best not to pretend otherwise. This would, however, exclude at least half of the prisoner-learners we met from participation, unless in their own time and at their own expense.

If, on the other hand, education and training are perceived as a central plank of the resettlement strategy for any prisoner, then significant additional resources will need to be devoted to making this a reality across the prison estate. Once this happened, education would move up the agenda, and new ways would be found of delivering education and training at different times and in different ways, to engage prisoner-learners, and make the activity meaningful.

Wider dimensions of the 'learning revolution' in the community as a whole, stressing the importance of seeing learning as truly 'life-long', indicate that this is the way things should be going in prison too. As the Chief Inspector of Prisons has commented, however, so much in prisons seems to be going on in 'virtual reality'. Prisons really are 'total institutions,' and revolutions in social attitudes, educational thinking and governmental policy alike commonly pass them by.

Group members expressed the wish to...

> *'bring everything up to date with what's happening in society'* (local).

One prisoner expressed the same point eloquently:

> *'It should be [seen as] education for young men or young women. It shouldn't be education "for prisoners".'* (C Cat training NIE)

Recommendations

The starting point for *Time to Learn* was to find out from prisoner-learners their views on prison education in order to inform improvements in policy and practice. The report demonstrates the value of involving prisoners in decisions regarding the planning and delivery of services.

Prison educators and policy makers are already aware of some of the concerns raised by the prisoners: gaps between prison and mainstream education; discontinuity between prisons, ranging from wide variations in resources to misplaced documentation; and a failure to connect learning in prison with educational opportunities after release. Some of the problems are already being tackled as part of the OLSU delivery plan, or will be in the near future. But this report adds new insights into a range of issues as perceived by the prisoner-learner.

The recommendations include the need for changes in policy and culture across the prison estate as well as changes on a more practical level, which may be implemented locally. They accord with the OLSU delivery plan and the recommendations put forward by the Social Exclusion Unit in its report on reducing re-offending by ex-prisoners.

Seven major recommendations are presented first. These are followed by more detailed recommendations relating to headings contained in part two of the report.

Principle Recommendations

1. Education and training should be integral to the resettlement of prisoners and its important contribution towards the Prison Service aim of reducing offending should be recognised.

2. Opportunities for education and training should be made available to all prisoners. The resources available should be comparable with those in mainstream provision, including supervised access to the Internet. Education and training should have equal status with offending behaviour and other correctional programmes. Targets for education and training should be agreed with individual prisoners and included in their sentence plans.

3. Rates of pay for prisoners attending education and training should be comparable with the rates of pay for other work. Comparable pay levels would help to ensure that education and training are seen as being at least as valued as other work activities within the prison regime.

4. A strategy should be devised nationally to identify the key barriers to learning in prison and to eliminate them. OLSU should take a lead role in addressing the problems of discontinuity identified in this report.

5. The curriculum should be of equal relevance to the needs of all prisoners, taking into account the massive range of different abilities, motivation, prior learning experience and attainment as well as the particular needs of certain groups, e.g. black and minority ethnic prisoners, women prisoners, young prisoners, prisoners serving long and short sentences, prisoners on remand and prisoners who have rejected the more traditional forms of education.

6. To maximise opportunities for learning, the OLSU should champion, and fund best practice in, the more flexible forms of provision, e.g. self study groups, distance and open learning, peer education, individual and peer supported cell work, prison officer supported cell study and study on the wings, and evening classes.

7.   Education consultative groups should be established and meet regularly to consider all aspects of the provision, from planning to delivery. The consultative groups should include learners and prisoners not in education and explore issues such as:

- barriers to learning and access to education
- curriculum and resources
- sentence planning
- learning contracts
- providing relevant education for specific groups, including prisoners from black and minority ethnic groups, older prisoners, vulnerable prisoners and those with learning disabilities, and
- events to celebrate learning achievements.

The consultative group could also be responsible for monitoring and reporting on the transfer of prisoners' education records and the use of learning passports (see recommendations 17 and 18) and the ongoing monitoring and assessment of provision.

Detailed recommendations

8.   Standards for prisoner education and training should be set in consultation with key stakeholder groups, including prisoners, educationalists, prison staff and relevant independent groups such as the Prisoners' Education Forum, the Prison Reform Trust and the Prisoners' Education Trust.

Curriculum

The OLSU delivery plan commits to 'undertaking a major review of the curriculum'. The following recommendations are made with this in mind:

9.   OLSU consultation with key stakeholder groups, including prisoners, educationalists, prison staff and relevant independent groups such as the Prison Reform Trust, the Prisoners' Education Forum and the Prisoners' Education Trust should be integral to the curriculum review process.

10. The core curriculum for education and training should provide a framework that ensures a degree of consistency of provision between prisons, in particular between prisons of the same/similar security categories. However, this should not limit the ability of individual prison education departments to respond to the particular needs of certain prisoners or to introduce flexible approaches to the delivery of learning provision.

Structure

11. Funding between prisons with similar roles should be made equitable. The OLSU should develop a rationale for education funding per head of prison population taking into account the different security categories and lengths of stay. Pre-existing inequalities of resources, for example IT equipment, should be rectified outside the adoption of any funding formula.

12. Key performance indicators for education and training should be based on the progression of individual prisoner-learners and not on absolute performance as measured by exam results.

13.   Induction and assessment

A standard assessment for educational needs should be adopted and implemented across the prison estate. The findings from this assessment should be used to inform decisions made between the prisoner and education staff about which learning opportunities he/she will participate in. The educational assessment should be integral to the new Offender Assessment System, OASys, which seeks to better inform sentence planning.

14.   *Applications for classes*

Each prison education department should develop, agree with other relevant prison staff and publish a transparent application process. A copy should be given to prisoners at induction and posted on notice boards on the wings and in the education department. The application process should include written feedback to the prisoner making the application and be concluded within a nationally agreed timeframe.

15.   *Waiting lists*

To reduce waiting times for prisoners wishing to access education and training generally and the more popular classes in particular, e.g. IT, vocational training and cookery, learning provision should be increased. The introduction of maximum waiting times to access education and training included as targets in sentence plans should be considered.

16.   *Regimes, timetabling and trade-offs*

In managing prison regimes, prison staff should ensure that prisoner-learners enjoy equity of provision with other prisoners in terms of opportunities to access the gym and the library, to join in association, to have a shower and go to the toilet. Prisoner-learners wishing to study in their cell should, in the absence of single cells, be paired with other learners.

17.   *Transfer of prisoners' education records*

The OLSU should consult with education managers and agree an IT based system and contents list for education records, to which the prisoner-learner would have access, and a timeframe within which the transfer of records should take place, following the move of the individual prisoner-learner between prisons.

18.   *Personal records*

Personal records of achievement or 'learning passports' should be introduced and maintained by prisoner-learners, supported and encouraged by education staff, personal officers and probation officers. Learning passports would include personal and sentence plan targets for education and training (see recommendation 2), records of achievement and progress verified by education staff and a copy of the individual prisoner-learner's standard assessment for educational needs (see recommendation 13). The concept of the learning passport should be considered as a personal record for the offender to include all learning undertaken under the auspices of the OLSU, e.g. including offending behaviour and other correctional programmes.

19.   *Encouraging access to learning*

The OLSU should champion and fund best practice that encourages those prisoners who have rejected the more traditional forms of education. In particular, the more imaginative blends of learning provision, e.g. the overlaying of creative arts classes and vocational training workshops or attendance at gym with the basic and key skills, flexible learning (see recommendation 6) should be encouraged.

20. *Involvement of outside agencies*

Ways in which charities and voluntary organisations can encourage and enhance learning, for example Toe by Toe and the Inside Out Trust should be disseminated by the OLSU and their involvement encouraged.

21. *Volumetric control*

Prisoner-learners' own educational records, books and study materials should be removed from the restrictions of volumetric control.

22. *Libraries*

Libraries should be readily accessible to prisoner-learners on a daily basis. All prisoners should have guaranteed access on a weekly basis. Strong links between education and library staff should be developed, including shared decisions relating to library procurement of educational texts, videos and CDs.

23. *Tutors, teaching style and inspection*

Throughout our study we heard much about the central importance of prison education staff. Prisoner-learners told us about the positive impact some members of education staff had on their motivation and learning, often beyond the boundaries of the classroom or subject being studied. The importance of staff-prisoner relationships leads to the following:

- The recruitment and retention of high quality prison education staff should be a priority for both education providers and the OLSU.
- All prison education staff should be supported by, and be required to participate in, annual programmes for continuing professional development.
- Accredited training modules for prison education staff and for those interested in teaching in prison should be further developed and made available through continuing professional development and initial teacher training.
- Initial training, for those new to the prison environment, should be developed and implemented for newly appointed prison education staff who have not previously taught in prison.
- Advanced practitioner status should be awarded to exceptional education staff, funded by the OLSU, and best practice shared through annual programmes for continuing professional development.
- Standards should be maintained within the framework of a rigorous and independent process of inspection.

People issues

24. *Family and friends*

The involvement of family and friends in supporting education and training should be encouraged. Examples of good practice should be shared, e.g. events to celebrate educational achievement, prisoners' writing and recording stories for their children, displays and art exhibitions staged in the visitors' centre.

25. *Prison officers*

The potential contribution of prison officers to education and training, and to the effective rehabilitation and resettlement of offenders should be highlighted in recruitment information and further reinforced during prison officer training. Further opportunities for job-related training, career and personal development should be made available for prison officers. Ways in which prison officers can contribute towards encouraging and supporting learning opportunities for prisoners should be the subject of further research.

26. *Education 'champions'*

Prison officer 'education champions' for each wing should be recruited, trained and supported by education managers in order to enhance, encourage and support learning opportunities for prisoners on the wings, including cell study. Opportunities for appropriately trained prison officers to support the work of the education department in other ways should be explored.

27. *Prison governors*

Prison governors should encourage and join in events to celebrate the achievements of prisoner-learners in education and training.

28. *Further research*

The concept of the prison as a learning environment for prisoners and staff should be the subject for further research and development.

29. *Release and resettlement*

Support for prisoner-learners wishing to continue with education and training on release should be made available before and after release, so providing a 'bridge' between learning in prison and the wider community. Support should come from a designated worker, ideally situated in the community to which the prisoner will be released. In many prisons, prison education staff help prisoner-learners interested in pursuing a course of study on release. This support should not be lost and close liaison between the prisoner-learner, education staff and designated worker should exist at all times.

30. *Encouraging learning in prison*

The role of wing education representative, similar to that undertaken by prisoners acting as race relations or diversity representatives should be established. The role would include the championing of education and training, and raising issues of interest or concern with the education department. An education and training working group or board could also be established to discuss and progress relevant issues. Such a body would be made up of representatives from the education department, prison staff (see recommendation 27) and the education consultative group (see recommendation 7).

31. *Learning from each other*

The OLSU should develop more practical ways for education staff, prison staff and providers of education to learn from each other. Networking between education staff across the prison estate and between education providers should be encouraged.

32. *Regular consultation*

The OLSU and providers of education should consult regularly with prisoner-learners, through education consultative groups, with education representatives (see recommendations 7 and 31), education staff, prison staff (see recommendation 26) and governors on the quality, quantity and relevance of learning provision. An electronic 'suggestions box' should be established, run and monitored by the OLSU, accessible to prisoner-learners, education and prison staff. Appropriate rewards for suggestions taken forward should be made.

REFERENCES

Braggins, J. (2002) *Shared Responsibilities: Education for prisoners at a time of change*, NATFHE and the Association of Colleges.

Dearing, R. (2002) 'Education should be the key to prisoners' freedom,' The Independent, 25 July 2002

.DfES (2001) Statistical Bulletin, 'Education and Training Expenditure since 1991-1992'.

DfES (2002) 'Education and Skills: Delivering Results – A Strategy to 2006'.

DfES/PLSU (2003) *Improving Offenders' Learning and Skills Delivery Plan 2003/4 – 2004/5.*

DfES (2003) *14-19: opportunities and excellence*, DfES.

Flynn, N. and Price, D., (1995) *'Education in Prisons – A National Survey'*, Prison Reform Trust.

Gosse, C. (2002) *Is education valued in prisons?* unpublished MA thesis, University of Southampton.

Home Office (2002) Prison Statistics England and Wales 2000, 2001.

Offenders Learning and Skills Unit website (2003) 'Initiatives: Curriculum, Key Facts,' (see also: Prison Service Order 4205, June 2000).

OLSU website, 'Initiatives: Basic Skills, Key Facts.'

PLSU (2002) 'Prisoners' Learning and Skills Delivery Plan: Executive Summary'.

RDS (2002) 'Prison Population Brief, England and Wales, December 2002,' Veronica Hollis and Michelle Goodman, London: Home Office.

RDS (2002) *Projections of long term trends in the prison population to 2009*, Rachel Councell and John Simes, National Statistics, Research, Development and Statistics Directorate, Home Office.

Social Exclusion Unit (2002) *Reducing re-offending by ex-prisoners*, London: SEU.

Tomlinson, M. (2003) 'Learning for all: can it be made a reality?' RSA Journal, June 2003.

Wilson, D. (2001) 'Valuing prisoner education, 'Prison Report, No. 54, 18-19.

Wilson, D. and Reuss, A., eds (2000) *Prison(er) Education: Stories of Change and Transformation*, Winchester: Waterside Press.

APPENDIX 1:
Advisory Group Membership

Professor Gus John	Chair of the Advisory Group Chair and Chief Executive, The Gus John Partnership Limited
Judith Williams	Chief Education Officer, Offenders Learning and Skills Unit
Catherine Atthill	Prisoners' Education Trust
Bob Shepherd	Key Skills Development Co-ordinator, Inside Out Trust
Chris Brimecombe	Head of Education, HMP Channings Wood
Emma Hughes	Treasurer, Forum on Prisoners' Education
Bill Duff	London Area Manager, HM Prison Service
Angela Neustatter	Journalist, author

APPENDIX 2

Time to Learn: Questionnaire

PRISON: _____

PRISON TYPE AND POPULATION: _____

EDUCATION CONTRACTOR: _____

GROUP SIZE: _____

_____HOW SELECTED? _____

INTERVIEWER: _____NOTE TAKER: _____

DATE: _____

_____

Introduction

Thank you for agreeing to take part in our survey. (Introduce self and colleague.) The survey is being conducted independent of the prison service by the PRT. A report will be published later this year and will present prisoners views and experiences of education in prison and make some important recommendations to the Prison Service and Government ministers. Although we are going to make notes of what you say, your names will not be used and everything you say will be treated in confidence. There are only 2 exceptions to this:

- anything someone says that suggests they are intending to hurt themselves or someone else, and
- anything we are legally obliged to report will be passed on.

I would of course discuss it with you first.

I asked to speak with you because I wanted to find out your thoughts about, and experiences of, prison education.

Do you have any questions before we begin? (Ask everyone to introduce themselves.)

Warm up

Which classes are you doing at the moment?

Have you done any other classes either at this prison or at another prison?

Have you gained any qualifications while you have been in prison?

What do you like most about going to education?

What do you like the least?

Are you doing anything else educational? (e.g. distance learning, one to one, cell work – what?)

How important is it?

Why have you enrolled for classes whilst you've been in prison?

What are the most important things you want to get out of your time in classes?

Help with reading and writing?

Help with maths?

Qualifications? Which?

Help to get a job?

To pass the time?

To gain new interests?

Other things? What? i.e. it helps with parole, gets you out of your cell

Do you think other people in prison want the same things as you from education?

If not, what else do you think they might want?

Do you think the people who work in prison think education for prisoners is important?

Using the following rating, how important do you think prison officers think education is? 1 = very important; 2 = important; 3 = indifferent and 4 = not important. Why? Ask for examples to illuminate responses and what students would want people who work in prison "to do" to improve the situation.

1   2   3   4

Using the same rating (and again, asking "why?" and for examples) how important do you think other staff in prison think education is? For example:

Workshop staff?

1   2   3   4

Probation officers?

1   2   3   4

Governors?

1   2   3   4

How important do you think education is?

1   2   3   4

How important do your family, girl/boyfriend, husband/wife think education is?

1   2   3   4

What's on offer?

How was it decided which class(es) you would attend in this prison? Explore the process from induction to attendance. Were your needs assessed?

Did you decide for yourself what you wanted? OR

Did somebody else decide for you?

If yes, explore what happened

What was it like getting onto the classes/courses you wanted, (was it easy or difficult)?

If you have been in another prison as part of this sentence was there any follow through, or did you have to start again in this prison?

Do you have a sentence plan?

If yes, is education part of it?

Are there any other classes you would like to see available?

If yes, what and why?

Has anyone here done a correspondence course (distance learning) in prison? Is it possible to do them in this prison?

Are there any IT/computer classes available in this prison?

Explore availability and prisoner opinion of

Can you study anywhere else other than in education classes, for example on the wings or in workshops?

If yes, how does this work? Does anyone help? Explore

Facilities, teaching and learning preferences (and links to experiences at school)

What was school like for you? Explore prior learning experience

Did you go to college or any sort of education after you left school?

If yes, what was that like? Continue to explore prior learning experience

How does your learning experience in prison compare?

When you go to a class, what are the things that help you learn?

 Which of the following, if any matters to you? Rate them in the following way: 1 = matters a lot; 2 = matters quite a lot; 3 = indifferent and 4 = doesn't matter at all

Class numbers (preference for smaller or larger classes)
1   2   3   4

Standard of class room materials and furnishing (ask about IT here)
1   2   3   4

Access to the library and availability of relevant books
1   2   3   4

Group discussion
1   2   3   4

Tutor
1   2   3   4

Interest in the subject
1   2   3   4

The thought that it might help to get a qualification

1   2   3   4

The thought that it might help to get a job on release
1   2   3   4

Getting to classes on time or at all i.e. prison officer escort
1   2   3   4

Personal choice
1   2   3   4

Anything else?

Barriers and opportunities

What encouraged you to attend education? Did anyone encourage you to attend?

Did anything put you off doing education?

How much time is available for education? Are you having to choose between either doing education or other activities i.e. ETS (enhanced thinking skills), Offending Behaviour programmes, work, gym, vocational training?

If yes, how difficult is that, how do you decide?

Do you think other activities are seen as more important than education? And if so what, by whom?

Are there waiting lists for some classes? If yes, which?

Do some prisoners get priority? Which ones? Why?

Does the prison consider some classes as more important than others? If yes, which?

What happens if you are transferred part way through a course?

Can you continue the course at the new prison?

Are your educational needs assessed again?

Thinking about other prisoners, do the classes suit everyone, or are some groups left out or given greater priority? (Note, not all questions will be relevant in all prisons)

Are there too many/not enough classes for literacy/basic skills?

Are there too many/not enough classes for:

Older or younger prisoners?

Sentenced or remand prisoners?

Vulnerable prisoners?

Short or long sentence prisoners?

Black and minority ethnic prisoners?

Others in this prison? Who?

Are there classes specially for prisoners who are also foreign nationals/don't speak English as their first language?

In women's prisons, are there classes that particularly support the needs of women?

How does this compare with other prisons you may have been in?

On release

Do you think that having attended classes while in prison will help you on release?

If yes, in what way?

If no, why not?

Thinking about your release, would you like to continue with some sort of education or training?

If yes, do you think this will be easy or difficult to arrange? Why?

And finally

Do you think that education in prison should be a right or a privilege?

In this prison, do you think prison staff think education is a right or a privilege?

Thinking about education overall, both inside prison and out – what, if anything has it got to offer you? What is it that you really want from education?

If you could change one thing about education for prisoners in general, what would it be? (Go round the group and ask for one thing from each prisoner)

Thank you for taking part. Any questions or comments?

Julia Braggins and Jenny Talbot
Prison Reform Trust

Appendix 3

List of prisons approached by name, type, CNA and region

Askham Grange
Female, open, training 139, (Yorkshire)

Aylesbury
Long term Young Offender Institution, 348, (Bucks)

Canterbury
Adult male, local, 196, (Kent)

Downview
Female, closed, 327, (South)

Glen Parva
Young offender, sentenced and remand, 664, (East Midlands)

Guys Marsh
Closed adult male and young offender, Cat C, 487, (South west)

Leicester
Adult male, local, Cat B, 219, (East Midlands)

Long Lartin
Adult male, training/dispersal, 522, (West Midlands)

Manchester
Adult male, local, 950, (North west)

Parc
Adult male and young offender, Cat B, local, 800,
(South Wales) Private prison

Pentonville
Adult male, local, 897, (London)

Send
Female, closed, 220, (South)

Swaleside
Adult sentenced male, 775, (Kent)

Wakefield
Adult male, dispersal, lifer main center, 585, (Yorkshire)

Wellingborough
Adult sentenced male, training, Cat C, 526, (East Midlands)

Note: Prison descriptors taken from HMP Service website, 7 February 2003.

APPENDIX FOUR

Research Team

Two Research Associates, Julia Braggins and Jenny Talbot, undertook the study on behalf of PRT. Both work as freelance researchers, consultants and trainers.

Julia Braggins has a long track record in the field of criminal justice. Until 1999 she was Director of the Centre for Crime and Justice Studies and editor of its quarterly magazine, 'Criminal Justice Matters'. Before that she worked in prison education, adult community education and the Open University.

Jenny Talbot's background is largely in the voluntary sector. Until last year she was Chief Executive of the Institute for Citizenship and before that Regional Director and co-founder of Common Purpose, a national charity running leadership development programmes for city decision makers aimed at enhancing multi-sector partnerships and co-operative working.

The researchers were assisted in the data gathering by Cecilia Yardley, a PRT volunteer, who conducted a search of background literature and assisted in taking notes at some of the prisons.